EVIL DOESN'T LIVE HERE
POSTERS FROM THE BOSNIAN WAR

За листу маршала Тита
ЗА БРАТСТВО И ЈЕДИНСТВО
НАРОДА ЈУГОСЛАВИЈЕ

EVIL DOESN'T LIVE HERE
POSTERS FROM THE BOSNIAN WAR

DAOUD SARHANDI & ALINA BOBOC
FOREWORD BY DAVID ROHDE

LAURENCE KING

PUBLISHED IN 2001 BY
LAURENCE KING PUBLISHING LTD
71 GREAT RUSSELL STREET
LONDON   WCIB 3BP
TEL: +44 020 7430 8850
FAX: +44 020 7430 8880
EMAIL: enquiries@laurenceking.co.uk
www.laurenceking.co.uk

PROJECT EDITOR: MARK LAMSTER
ADDITIONAL EDITING: NICOLA BEDNAREK AND LINDA LEE
BOOK DESIGN: ETAL-DESIGN.COM/PRINCETON
ARCHITECTURAL PRESS/EVAN SCHONINGER
COVER DESIGN: DEB WOOD

PAGE 2: BRANKA HEGEDUŠIĆ, *FOR BROTHERHOOD AND UNITY*, 1945. SIX WOMEN REPRESENT THE REPUBLICS OF YUGOSLAVIA: BOSNIA-HERZEGOVINA, CROATIA, MACEDO-NIA, MONTENEGRO, SERBIA, AND SLOVENIA.

PRINTED AND BOUND IN SINGAPORE.

A CATALOGUE RECORD FOR THIS BOOK IS AVAILABLE
FROM THE BRITISH LIBRARY.
ISBN 1 85669 263 9

CONTENTS

BOSNIA-HERZEGOVINA

DANUBE

SAVA

CROATIA

• ZAGREB

OSIJEK •

VUKOVAR •

NOVI SAD •

• SLAVONSKI BROD

• PRIJEDOR

• BIHAĆ

BRČKO

• BEJELJINA

BELGRADE

BANJA LUKA
•

TUZLA •

• JAJCE

ZENICA

DRINA

SREBRENICA

• TRAVNIK

ŽEPA •

KUPRES

SARAJEVO • PALE

DRINA

ADRIATIC SEA

• SPLIT

GORAŽDE

FOČA

FEDERAL REPUBLIC
OF YUGOSLAVIA

• MOSTAR

DUBROVNIK •

- - - - EXTERNAL BORDER AGREED
AT THE UNITED NATIONS,
MAY 21, 1992.

——— BOUNDARY LINE
AGREED AT DAYTON,
NOVEMBER 21, 1995.

SERB REPUBLIC
49% OF BOSNIA

FEDERATION OF
BOSNIA-HERZEGOVINA
51% OF BOSNIA

FOREWORD
DAVID ROHDE

From 1992 to 1995, the combatants in the war in Bosnia used posters in a desperate struggle to rally their people and shape international opinion. Some of their causes were just, such as the Bosnian government's stated goal of fostering a multiethnic society. Others, such as Serb and Croat nationalist drives to create ethnically pure republics, were repugnant. But the imagery and wordplay on all sides was potent and often had destructive consequences. The posters skillfully compiled here by Daoud Sarhandi testify to the power of that visual communication.

While covering the war for the *Christian Science Monitor*, I experienced the power of propaganda campaigns firsthand. I remember interviewing a Serb soldier manning an artillery position high above the besieged city of Sarajevo in 1995. I asked him why he was fighting. The soldier replied that he was doing battle for his wife and daughter. If the Islamic fundamentalists in Sarajevo won control of the country, he explained, his wife and daughter would be forced to wear veils and would be barred from driving. It would be like Saudi Arabia, he said. He was utterly wrong. Of the three sides in the war, the Bosnian Muslim authorities were the most tolerant. But the soldier was so saturated with propaganda that he earnestly believed his own words. Later in the war, a young Serb woman living outside Sarajevo told me vehemently that Muslims had dynamited the Serbian Orthodox church in that city. I reassured her that I had been in Sarajevo a few days earlier and that the church was still standing. I had been tricked, she insisted, convinced that it lay in ruins.

The Bosnian War was not the product of "ancient ethnic hatreds." Neighbor did not suddenly and savagely turn upon neighbor. The bloodletting came after ultra-nationalists mounted massive propaganda campaigns to incite fear and hatred. That was the tragedy of the war. Propaganda twisted perception, transforming neighbors into sworn enemies and innocent civilians into targets. I left Bosnia deeply shaken by the power of propaganda and by the ability of ordinary people to rationalize their actions, no matter how brutal.

Evil Doesn't Live Here is a fascinating study of the visual communication generated by the Bosnian War. Most of the posters on these pages are testaments to human creativity and tolerance. Others speak to our darker side. Taken together, they force us to ask difficult questions about the nature of art, graphic design, and propaganda—and the roles each played in a conflict that was both tragic and preventable.

ACKNOWLEDGMENTS

First among those who made this book possible are Rupert Wolfe Murray and Stephanie Wolfe Murray, who believed in and backed the project consistently from its inception. Special thanks also go to Steven Gordon, who photographed the posters in often difficult circumstances. At etal-design.com, Sue Smallwood showed dedication and care in designing this book, and Phil Cleaver was committed to it throughout the design period. At Princeton Architectural Press, Mark Lamster finally made it happen.

The many artists and designers whose posters appear throughout this book are credited where appropriate and listed at the back. It goes without saying that without their generous consent to allow us to reproduce their work, there would be no book.

We would like to express our gratitude to the following individuals and organizations in Bosnia who assisted us with our research:

Tuzla: Dom Armije, Sanjin Memišević, the Tuzla Citizens' Forum, Printcom, Ratna Štamparija, Sinan Alić at Ogledalo, Fatmir Alispahić at the Opština Press Centre.

Sarajevo: Amra Zulfikarpašić at the Academy of Art, Dajana Rešić, Press Centre-Dom Armije, Alma Duraković and Snježana Mulić at Dani, Ermin Sarajlija at the Human Rights Centre-University of Sarajevo, Ibrahim Spahić at the International Peace Centre, Seid Hasanefendić and Ivana Jevdjević at the National Gallery, Seada Hadžimehmedagić at the Archive of Bosnia-Herzegovina, Emir Čengić at ULUPUBIH, Edin Numankadić, Kamerni Theatre, FAMA, and Zlatan Ibrahimpašić.

Travnik: Jasmina Hopić at the Archive of Central Bosnia.
Zenica: Radovan Marušić at the National Theatre.
Mostar: Zlatko Serdarević at RTV Mostar.
Banja Luka: Ljiljana Misirlić at Dom Kulture, Saša Grubac, Miloš Šolaja at the Press Club, Verica Stošić and Ljubica Ječimović at the Archive of Republika Srpska, Gradjanski Glas.
Bijeljina: Museum of Bijeljina.
Zagreb, Croatia: Dolores Ivanuša at the Croatian History Museum, Marijan Susovski at the Museum of Contemporary Art.
Serbia: Djorde Balmazović and Dragan Protić at Škart, Smiljka Kašić at the National Library of Serbia, Vladan Radosavljević at the Media Centre, Darka Radosavljević at Radio B92, FIA, Maja Marinković, Women in Black, Goranka Matić at Vreme, Milena Dragičević at the Faculty of Dramatic Art, the Centre of Contemporary Art-the Fund for an Open Society, Raša Todosijević, Saša Rakezić, Mihajlo Aćimović, Andrej Tišma, Miroslav Popović from Magnet, Zoran Pantelić from Absolutno. Special thanks to Mirko for the apartment and to Jelena, who showed us so much hospitality and whose friendship made our days in Belgrade so enjoyable.

Additional thanks go to: Magdalena Szczepaniak, Vesna Manojlović, Mary Sarhandi, Vesna Marić, Lilijan Sulejmanović, Monica Wolfe Murray, Paddy Cramsie, Steven Heller, Čedomir Kostović, Dino Omerović, Sanda Jelić, Jim Haynes, Jan Nuckowski.

ALL OF THE MATERIAL THAT WAS GIVEN TO
THE AUTHORS WAS SUBSEQUENTLY DONATED
TO THE ARCHIVE OF BOSNIA-HERZEGOVINA
IN SARAJEVO.

FOR SERBIA

Two of Serbia's nationalist politicians: opposition leader Vuk Drašković with President Slobodan Milošević pasted onto his body in Belgrade in 1998. *Photograph by Daoud Sarhandi.*

INTRODUCTION
DAOUD SARHANDI

My first trip to Bosnia came in October 1995, three months after the civilian massacres in Srebrenica. I wanted to do something, anything, to express my revulsion at what had happened there, to provide what little assistance I could, to demonstrate that I was not part of a world that had permitted or tacitly condoned such atrocities. And so I joined an aid organization based in Manchester and ended up driving to Tuzla, a town in northeast Bosnia within the Muslim-Croat Federation.[1]

The idea for this book came in Tuzla just over two years later. On my fourth trip to the town, in the autumn of 1997, I visited Jasminko Arnautović, a prolific designer of antinationalist posters. While looking at Arnautović's work—some of which is reproduced here—I talked with him about the information battle that had been waged for the hearts and minds of the Bosnian people. It was then that I realized that a collection of posters would produce a fascinating insight into how the Bosnian people were addressed, by whom, and to what ends during the conflict there. I felt sure that it would also produce an interesting portrait of how they responded, intellectually and emotionally, to the conflict that surrounded them. *Evil Doesn't Live Here* focuses on posters that were produced between the start of the Bosnian War in April 1992 and its end in 1995, after a peace agreement was reached in Dayton, Ohio, between the presidents of Bosnia, Serbia, and Croatia.

Collecting the posters was no simple task; it took me (and my research assistant, Alina Boboc) one year between late 1997 and 1998. Research was performed under the most difficult conditions, and required countless trips across the war-torn country. Artists often worked alone, and many emigrated during the war, taking their work with them; most of these artists we managed to trace, some we could not. Very few printers kept copies of posters they had produced, although they often remembered them and pointed us in the right direction. Posters were generally printed in limited numbers, due to the material hardships that existed in towns and cities under siege, making them even harder to track down.[2]

More than six years after the end of the war, posters still play a vital role in the dissemination of information in Bosnia, particularly in regard to such important issues as refugees, freedom of movement, land mines, reconstruction, and politics. The United Nations, the OHR (Office of the High Representative, which holds responsibility for the civil implementation of the Dayton agreement), SFOR (the NATO-led Stabilization Force in Bosnia), the OSCE (Organization for Security and Cooperation in Europe), and various nongovernmental organizations all produce large amounts of public information. This material vies for the attention of the Bosnian people alongside posters produced by a dizzying number of political parties.

These three posters appeared in Tuzla in late 1998 prior to the Bosnian elections. The top is by Jasminko Arnautović and was produced for the Tuzla Citizens' Forum. Arnautović spells the "democracy" of 1990—which led to Bosnian independence—in human bones. The middle poster depicts Che Guevara, and the bottom one equates nationalism with war. *Photographs by Daoud Sarhandi.*

OPPOSITE:
FROM GREAT TO SMALL SERBIA
Maps of Greater Serbia started appearing in the late 1980s. This one, published in September 1991 in the ultranationalist publication *Pogledi*, covers most of Croatia and all of Bosnia.

Given these realities, we have also included key posters produced after the Dayton agreement, as well as several from before the outbreak of war in Bosnia. This last category includes a selection of posters that we unearthed in Croatia. These powerful images, created in 1991 during the Serb-Croat War, express sentiments and themes similar to those that later surfaced in Bosnia.

During the Bosnian War, posters became tremendously important. With normal channels of communication shut down, and no mass-media outlets, the only news available came by word of mouth and was often only about the immediate vicinity. In such an environment, posters were a cheap and effective way of disseminating information. Not surprisingly, poster "battles" took place in Bosnia. Rival ideological groups tore down each other's work, and tried to dominate the best sites. A town might awaken to see an entire area emblazoned with multiple copies of one poster, only to find them gone the next day, replaced by another creation. Posters were also pasted onto the sides of trucks and driven around. In Sarajevo, bill-posters were paid danger money to put up posters on the most lethal streets, such as the infamous Sniper Alley. This

was also an act of defiance, since places such as these were in the sights of besieging gunmen.

Poster designers came from all sectors of the artistic community and sometimes from outside it: there were professional graphic designers who had been working in artistic, cultural, and commercial fields before the war; fine artists who adapted their talents to the new reality; and amateur, or one-off, designers who were propelled toward design as a way of expressing themselves or serving their regiment or party.

In extreme situations posters were painted by hand. Mostly, however, they were printed by lithography or silkscreen—the latter being more common. Beyond the artistic merits of silkscreening, lithographic plates were in short supply during the war, and there was often no electricity to run the presses they required. Silkscreens also had the advantage of being recyclable—once the embedded image was washed away, screens could be reused for other work. For all these reasons, original plates of the posters that were produced during the war are hard to find.

Since the end of World War II, poster art has played a significant role in Central and Eastern European politics, due to the nature of socialism and the various countries' dependence on Soviet-style propaganda techniques. Posters were originally used by socialist states to mark anniversaries and deliver simple sociopolitical statements. With the death of Stalin, poster art began to mature. Although posters were still commissioned for ideological purposes—for which artists were well paid—states were becoming more interested in the power of television, and kept an increasingly watchful eye on the "serious arts": painting, sculpture, film, and theater. New designers were coming out of art schools, and together with their elders they began to devote their talents to the cultural life of their countries. Posters started to develop along different lines, but as long as they were not openly confrontational, their designers were left pretty much alone.

Many of the works in this volume owe something to postwar Polish poster design—in particular its visual playfulness, stark simplicity, and directness, especially when dealing with painful subjects. Like Polish posters, many of the posters from the Bosnian War use strong symbolism and minimalist typography.[3] Despite the totalitarian regime of postwar Poland, though, the intent of these posters is obviously very different. The mood in many of the Bosnian posters is one of desperation and bitter cynicism: bullet holes, blood, and Serbian slogans juxtaposed with the Nazi swastika. Bosnians are notorious for their sharp, irreverent sense of humor, and these posters are often characterized by wry, black comedy as well.

When looking through this collection, one is struck by the diversity of the work. The artists' sheer eclecticism, combined with their emotional commitment, impresses most of all.

Balkan politics have a reputation for being impenetrably complex. In some ways this is true, and it stems from the fact that for centuries foreign interests have overlapped and competed in the region. Tragically, this complexity was used as a veil to obscure the basic facts about the fracture of the former Yugoslavia and the wars that enveloped the region during the 1990s. Issues were deliberately clouded. A campaign of misinformation was orchestrated by the dominant powers in Yugoslavia several years before war broke out. It spread and intensified during the military campaigns and persists, in some forms, to this day. For this reason, it is necessary to review, simply and concisely, the primary causes and outcomes of the war in Bosnia. Although the object of this book is to tell a visual story, an account of the events that took place is critical in order to understand the subject and appreciate the works illustrated here.

Although there are civil dimensions to most wars fought within a single country's borders, the Bosnian War was not a civil war, though it has often been described as one. Nor did it erupt spontaneously because of irreconcilable differences between the ethnic and religious groups that inhabit Bosnia-Herzegovina. These facts cannot be repeated often enough, especially since for most of the war large swaths of the foreign media, especially those who never visited the region, simply missed the conflict's real causes, and instead perpetuated a story of warring factions and ancient ethnic hatreds. Although there were many fine journalists working on the ground in Bosnia—some of whom lost their lives in the conflicts in Bosnia and Croatia—this version of events, initially put forward by ill-informed Western statesmen, was repeated so frequently and by so many that over time it achieved the status of historical truth. The facts about the causes of the war in Bosnia are very different, however, and these popular representations of the conflict have been extremely destructive. They played straight into the hands of the aggressors by masking their intentions and the precise nature of their involvement. Indeed, this misinformation was often used as a justification by the aggressors themselves. The effect was that all groups were portrayed as simply barbaric, robbing the story of its legitimate political context and perhaps even protracting the suffering.

Although ethnic hatreds in Bosnia developed and became more entrenched during the course of the war, the war simply could not and would not have happened without the instigation of Serbian and Croatian leaders. Presidents Slobodan Milošević in Serbia and Franjo Tudjman in Croatia—along with a supporting cast of nationalists in both countries— deserve the blame for the tragedies that have befallen the people of Bosnia-Herzegovina and the rest of the former Yugoslavia.[4]

National identity was always a topic of currency in Yugoslavia. Polls were taken about real and perceived nationality on a regular basis. To pretend that any of the republics, including Bosnia-Herzegovina, was ever a happy melting pot of its constituent nationalities is fanciful. Tensions did exist. But it was not until the mid-eighties, when Yugoslavia began to lose its strategic Cold War importance and its economy started to crumble, that powerful and dangerous nationalist sentiments were revived by leading academics in Serbia.[5]

At first Milošević, still a loyal Communist, condemned this overt nationalism. Later, however, when he realized that he could harness the forces of Serbian nationalism to his advantage, he began to promote this ideology, playing on and exacerbating the existing tensions, spreading first mistrust, then fear, and finally hatred.

KOSOVO'S GOLGOTHA

This magazine, from October 1988, is a *Politika* news group publication, and uses a familiar emotive image to illustrate a contemporary news story. The source and meaning of the original picture is unknown, but it is related to the idea that Serbs are fighting for their lives.

SERBIA NEEDS YOUR HELP

In May 1992, as war in Bosnia was gaining pace, *Politika*—the main state news group in Serbia—reprinted three posters that were originally published in France during World War I, when Serbia and France were allies.

EXODUS—300 YEARS

The propaganda technique of linking past and present conflicts has been used repeatedly in Serbia to propagate myths of Serb persecution. This powerful cover from the Serbian magazine *NIN*—another from the state-run *Politika* news group—combines a famous painting depicting the exodus of Serbs from Kosovo in 1689 with a protest march by Serbs from Kosovo to Belgrade. The march, organized by the Milošević regime, was itself a work of stage-managed propaganda.

OPPOSITE LEFT:

WE ARE BUILDING OUR SOCIETY TOGETHER
OSCE, 1996

The word "tolerance" in this poster is spelled with a combination of Latin and Cyrillic letters to emphasize unity.

OPPOSITE RIGHT:

WHO IS WHO?
Local Democracy Embassy
Tuzla, 1997

One of the few posters that refers to Bosnia's other main ethnic minorities, Roma and Jews.

Enemies were needed in the pursuit of a "Greater Serbia," and Milošević found them everywhere.

Kosovo was an early and important focus for the radicalization of Serbs as Milošević rose to power. Most Serbs consider Kosovo the ancient seat of their church and culture, and as early as 1987 Milošević incited the discontent of the Serb minority there by predicting impending war against non-Serbs, as if such an event were somehow predestined. At a rally in Kosovo in April 1987 he announced to the Serbian crowd, "It was never part of the Serbian and Montenegrin character to give up in the face of obstacles, to demobilize when it's time to fight." And again in Kosovo in 1989—celebrating the martyred defeat of Serbs at the hands of the Turks in 1389—he warned, "Six centuries later, we are again in battles and quarrels. They are not armed battles, though such things should not be excluded yet."[6] According to the Hague Tribunal's indictment of Milošević, in making statements such as these he "broke with the party and government policy which had restricted nationalist sentiment in [Yugoslavia] since the time of its founding by Josip Broz Tito."[7]

Revoking the autonomy of Kosovo and Vojvodina in 1989 was the first step in Milošević's plan to hijack the former Yugoslavia.[8] This act gave him far greater control over the country, since the federal presidency required eight votes to enact constitutional changes. Montenegro was already compliant with Milošević and so, along with the votes from Vojvodina and Kosovo, Serbia now controlled half of the eight votes. Abrogating the autonomy of these two provinces, however, led Slovenia and Croatia to fear for their own safety. Serbian-led actions and rising Serb nationalism prompted them to hold referenda, and when their populations voted to secede from Yugoslavia—as did the citizens of Bosnia and Macedonia in early 1992—Milošević's pseudo-constitutional takeover plan was finished. On June 28, 1991, war in Yugoslavia began.

Starting with Slovenia, Milošević attempted to grab as much of the country by force as he could using the armed might of the Yugoslav People's Army (*Jugoslovenska Narodna Armija* or JNA).[9] The JNA had been a pan-Yugoslav army, but by the end of the 1980s it had been purged to the extent that it was a Serb army, loyal only to Milošević and the idea of a dominant Serbia. After just ten days of botched fighting in Slovenia, the JNA moved against Croatia, precipitating a bloody conflict. As ugly as the war in Croatia was, however, its horrors were rapidly eclipsed by the carnage and destruction that would later overwhelm Bosnia-Herzegovina.

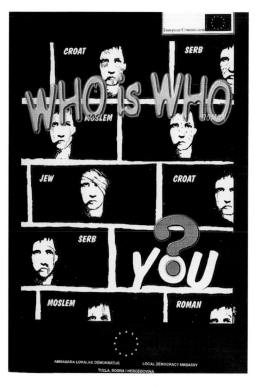

The wars in Croatia and Bosnia were fought on the shallow pretext that the Serbs who lived in those regions were in mortal danger from Croats and Muslims and should therefore be incorporated into an enlarged Serbian state. This nationalistic obsession with a Greater Serbia was far from new; it has a long history going back to at least the middle of the nineteenth century. The obsession, and the mythology that surrounds it, has been exploited by a succession of Serbian politicians, and the outcome has always been fatal. In the late 1980s, nationalism in Serbia stimulated nationalism in the other republics. Their nervous ethnic majorities provided the right political climate for other nationalist leaders, such as Franjo Tudjman in Croatia—and to a lesser extent presidents Milan Kučan in Slovenia and Alija Izetbegović in Bosnia—to step into the limelight and find their electorates. Once nationalists were elected by the republics' dominant ethnic groups, fear spread among the minorities; these fears were then exploited by their own ethnic leaders. It was a downward spiral of fear, counter-fear, and political opportunism that started in Serbia and spread across Yugoslavia. Though Milošević's nationalistic appeal to Serbs was greatly aided by the sabre-rattling of Tudjman, in the late eighties and early nineties neither Tudjman nor the presidents of the other republics had the means to start wars, even if they had wanted to do so. Bosnia's situation was always slightly different and potentially more explosive than those of the other republics. Although Bosniacs (Bosnian Muslims) were the largest single group in the country—constituting 44 percent of the population—Orthodox Serbs accounted for 33 percent and Catholic Croats for 17 percent. Jews, Turks, Roma, and other minorities made up the rest. Izetbegović, voted into power in 1990, was aware of the devastating consequences that war in Bosnia would have, and initially did everything in his power to prevent it. Although there were some UN peacekeepers in Sarajevo, Izetbegović implored the UN to deploy a larger, more robust force in the country. Although war was already raging in Croatia, and the political division of the population in Bosnia along ethnic lines had already taken place—with the Serb nationalist Radovan Karadžić wielding considerable political power and issuing apocalyptic warnings to the Muslims—Izetbegović's pleas fell, for the most part, on deaf ears.[10]

Dismembering a country with a population as ethnically entwined as Bosnia's was not easy. But the

FORMER YUGOSLAVIA

more interethnic brutality that occurred, the more it reinforced the notion that, for their own good, the three ethnic groups should not live together. This had the effect of making ethnic partition a seemingly unavoidable solution—and a stock gambit of all nationalists during the war. Although it was a powerful, well-equipped army, the JNA could not be relied on to perform the kind of brutality needed to accomplish this goal. So, covertly financed by Belgrade, paramilitary forces from Serbia were used: Šešelj's Četniks, Drašković's Serbian Guard, Arkan's infamous Tigers, and many other paramilitaries and local militias harassed, raped, and killed civilians. At the beginning of the war, particularly in eastern Bosnia, this was done easily, with little resistance. Later, paramilitaries were only sent in once Serb artillery had finished shelling population centers into submission.[11] This technique was perfected in Croatia and then used to devastating effect in Bosnia as well as Kosovo. Also, in the run up to the wars, local Serb civilians were given a twenty-four-hour diet of noxious propaganda from Belgrade. When the time came they were armed and incited to violence against their longtime neighbors. In Bosnia, Karadžić metamorphosed into a warlord under Serbia's patronage, and the Bosnian Serb Army was created out of civilians and units of the JNA to carry out his and Milošević's bidding.

The phrase "ethnic cleansing" was initially used by the media in Serbia to describe acts committed against Croats in areas of Croatia taken over during the Serb offensive. It has since entered the vocabularies of languages around the world. Although no side in the Bosnian War was entirely innocent of practicing such crimes, the elimination of minorities was never an official policy of the elected government in Sarajevo, nor was it routinely practiced by the Bosnian Army (ABiH).[12] Ethnic cleansing, however, very quickly became the raison d'être of Serb and Croat forces and their irregulars. Territorial domination in Bosnia—and the eventual assimilation of these areas—was the goal of the two leaders, and with their limited political vision, they saw territorial ethnic purity as their only means of achieving it. Ethnic purging of the areas they wished to control was a strategy, not a by-product, of the wars they waged.

Although Western powers were not the cause of the recent Balkan wars, there was an element of collusion between the leading nations and the instigators of the war. In their efforts to find the most expedient solution to the region's problems, some Western statesmen paraphrased and thereby legitimized the worst Balkan nationalists. This situation degenerated from essentially passive complicity to tragically active involvement when the UN Security Council, at the behest of its permanent members, insisted on enforcing an arms embargo against a legitimate UN member-state—Bosnia-Herzegovina—that patently needed to defend itself against overwhelming external force.[13] Under the guidance of Secretary General Boutros Boutros-Ghali and his special envoy Yasushi Akashi, the UN stood by and watched a massive displacement of civilians and the commission

ABOVE:
1ST COMMEMORATION SREBRENICA & ŽEPA
Fuad Kasumović
Tuzla, 1996
This poster marks the first anniversary of the falls of Srebrenica and Žepa. UNPROFOR has been crossed with the word "treason."

LEFT:
A SECURE FUTURE FOR CROATIA
HDZ
An election poster for Franjo Tudjman, president of Croatia between 1990 and 1999.

ABOVE:

IF THIS IS SOMEONE'S IDEA FOR
PEACE IN BOSNIA-HERZEGOVINA,
THEN MAYBE YOU SHOULD LISTEN TO
SOMEONE ELSE . . .
NATO
Sarajevo, 1996

This poster contained one of the strongest messages produced by the international community. The photograph shows fresh graves in a Sarajevan cemetery. The poster was designed by the NATO-led IFOR information department in support of the elections in September 1996. It was withdrawn after officials in the Republika Srpska complained that it was biased against Serbs.

OPPOSITE, LEFT TO RIGHT:
IMPOSSIBLE! ENOUGH!
FIA
Belgrade, 1992

This strange poster—produced in 1992 by the FIA art group in Belgrade—is one of the very few posters we found in Serbia that made any reference to the wars in the region.

ČETNIK WOODSTOCK

Vreme is the leading independent news magazine in Serbia. A photograph taken at a Serbian religious festival in the spring of 1998 illustrates the extent to which ultranationalism had become commonplace in Serbia. The Četniks were a royalist armed group that at various times in the region's history attempted to carve out a Greater Serbian kingdom. During World War II they committed appalling atrocities in Yugoslavia. Their ideas were revived recently, most notably by Vojislav Šešelj, leader of the ultranationalist Serb Radical Party.

THE TIGERS ARE COMING

A warning and a prophesy: The gangster and paramilitary leader Arkan—who did so much damage in Croatia, Bosnia, and Kosovo—is depicted on the cover of *NIN* in December 1991.

of war crimes on a scale not seen in Europe since the 1940s. For more than three years, European Union "observers," UN soldiers, and designated "safe areas" grudgingly coexisted with concentration and rape camps, as well as snipers who openly bragged that nimble Sarajevan children were a better test of their marksmanship than the elderly. The low point came in July 1995, when Serb forces walked into Srebrenica, rounded up between seven and eight thousand men and boys, and murdered them in cold blood. The UN, after having pledged to protect Srebrenica, did nothing.

There were no winners in Bosnia. Some 250,000 people died; more than two million were left homeless or displaced; a beautiful country was littered with mines, much of it reduced to rubble; and just about everyone was emotionally or physically scarred. Those deluded enough to claim some kind of victory actually gained nothing more than the right to live in morally bankrupt and economically unsustainable ghettos.

The NATO-enforced peace that holds in Bosnia is a fragile and artificial one with little or no real justice. Dangerous divisions exist between and within its two entities, the Muslim-Croat Federation and the Republika Srpska (Republic of Serbs).[14] Refugees of all nationalities are still unable to return to their homes, and indicted war criminals remain at large. Although the overall situation is improving incrementally, nationalism on all sides, but especially in Croat- and Serb-controlled areas, seems dug-in for the foreseeable future.

Immediately after the Dayton agreement was ratified, the British historian Noel Malcolm wrote:

> The new Bosnia, presaged by yesterday's peace accord signing in Paris, will be the geopolitical equivalent of an artwork by Damien Hirst. Hirst takes a cow, saws it in half, and pickles each half in formaldehyde. It may be an ingenious work of art, but is it still a cow? Similarly with the new Bosnia. It may have the cleverest of constitutions, but is it still a country?[15]

Although it took the convoy I was with more than two weeks to reach Tuzla from Britain on my first trip to Bosnia in October 1995, we could stay for only three days. I was therefore keen to return, to see people I had met, and to ensure donated television equipment I was responsible for reached its final destination: TV Tuzla. My return trip came in late December 1995. The Dayton agreement was coming into effect, and although the weather and the roads were punishing, it was easier to drive through Bosnia than it had been for years.

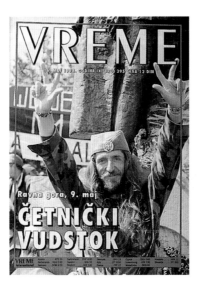
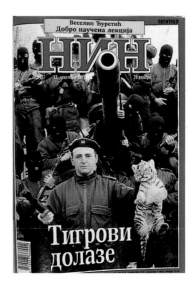

Roadblocks set up by the three indigenous armies had largely disappeared. Gone too were the red-and-green UNPROFOR (United Nations Protection Force) flags used to indicate the threat of sniper activity. Although the transition to the stronger, NATO-led Implementation Force (IFOR) was in full swing, we did not entirely trust the route through still-disputed, Serb-held territory around Sarajevo, and decided to enter Tuzla the way we knew, across snowy mountains and muddy tracks. This time I stayed on in Bosnia for several weeks, eager to see more of the country than I had in the autumn. I spent a couple of weeks in Tuzla, and then visited Sarajevo and Mostar.

Sarajevo was dotted with scores of fresh graves with simple markers bearing dates between 1992 and 1995. Sniper barricades constructed of wrecked cars sat in front of buildings and across bridges. The phrase *Pazi Snajper* ("Beware Sniper") was still scrawled on walls and nailed to trees. Mounds of rubbish lay uncollected everywhere. But amid the devastation, Sarajevans were becoming used to the idea that they could once again walk the streets of their city without fear of snipers. Whatever the terms of Dayton's divisive peace—and democratic Bosnians everywhere felt they were essentially unjust—Sarajevans were rejoicing.

If there is one place in Bosnia-Herzegovina that illustrates what has rightly been termed "urbicide," it is Mostar. Not content to eradicate its inhabitants, in 1993 the Tudjman-sponsored Croat forces (the HVO or Croatian Council of Defense) tried to erase the entire eastern (Muslim) side of the city.[16] The fate of the Stari Most (Old Bridge) is emblematic. This delicate, gracious bridge over the Neretva River was designed by the Turkish architect Hajrudin in 1566; it gave the city its name, linked its sides, and underpinned its identity. In 1992 the bridge was damaged by Serb forces, and late in the following year it was deliberately destroyed with one shell fired from a Croat tank. In a country once full of bridges, the Stari Most symbolized the relationship between Bosnia's eastern and western traditions, its various nationalities and faiths. Its unnecessary destruction had a predictable psychological effect.

I left Mostar through the almost completely unscathed west side of the city and drove up to Zagreb. My route took me through the town of Knin, and then on through a series of blackened ghost villages. This was the region that, in 1989, the media in Serbia began referring to as the *Serb Krajina*, or "Serb Border."[17] This poor part of Croatia was populated mainly by Serbs, and had been taken over by Serb paramilitaries in 1991 and purged of all Croats on the pretext that the Serbs who lived there—many for centuries—were in mortal danger in Tudjman's new Croatian state. When it was no longer politically expedient for Milošević to prop up this obviously criminal para-state—and he was looking for a way out of the quagmire of the wars he had started—the Krajina Serbs were abandoned to their fate. In July 1995 the area was "liberated" by Croatian forces in a U.S.-backed military operation that lasted just two days. It was appropriately code-named Storm, and resulted in the purging of the entire Serb population of nearly 200,000.

ЦРВЕНЕ Б

БРЧ

After returning to Britain I went to stay at a friend's cottage near Kendal in the Lake District. It was a hard winter and the region was frequently snowed in. One afternoon, while hiding from the cold in a local junk shop, I came across a box containing a jigsaw puzzle with an unidentified scenic view on the lid. The image and its identity took a few seconds to coalesce, but then it hit me. I was looking at a picture of Mostar: an inhabited, tranquil Mostar; a sunny Mostar with a bridge, bathers, and picturesque, ivy-clad houses with washing fluttering outside the windows. In short, a vanished Mostar. There is, of course, something strikingly apt about an image of Mostar as a jigsaw puzzle. Mostar is more brutally divided than any other place in Bosnia. Croatia effectively governs its Catholic west side, Bosnia its Muslim east side.

This puzzle metaphor can be extended to all of Bosnia. Glance at any recent map of the region and you will see a multicolored patchwork with population densities highlighted by ethnicity and nationality. The various factions have all generated maps indicating national territorial ambitions and counter-ambitions, with proposals for old and new ethnic divisions and internal borders. On the ground, borders in the form of front lines appeared in towns and cities and cut through villages. Driving around Bosnia during the war—and even long afterward—felt like driving across a huge puzzle. Although Serbia was the leader in the creation of maps of her "greater" territories—of which Bosnia was only a proposed part—the Croats joined the fray and, not to be outdone, the international community drafted its own lines across the country. As the journalist Anthony Borden wrote:

How many wasted hours must have been spent in the UN's Palais de Nations in Geneva, bent over diagrams of Bosnia's triangle shape, trying to envisage peace through colored pens. . . . Some gave more to "the Muslims," some gave more to "the Serbs," some gave dedicated territory to "the Croats," while others joined them with the Sarajevo government. What they all had in common is the link between ethnicity and territory.[18]

PREVIOUS PAGES:
THE RED BERETS OF BRČKO
A calendar produced in 1995 by the Serb army in Brčko. The detail at the top right shows Serb soldiers seated on the remains of a mosque. This calendar was found in the possession of a disabled Serbian boy who had lost his entire family in the fighting. In a musty apartment devoid of furniture, the boy showed us his military "archive" and shook his head; his face was grave as he told us that the war was simply a *katastrofa.*

MOSTAR
ABOVE: Jigsaw puzzle with image of Mostar and the Stari Most. *BELOW:* The destroyed Stari Most in January 1996. *Photograph by Daoud Sarhandi.*

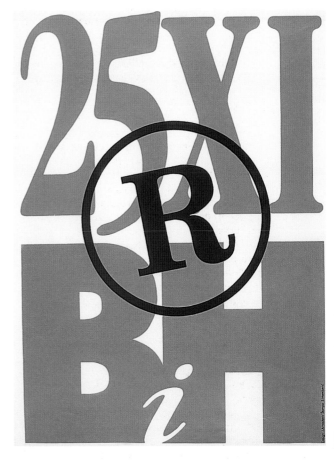

CLOCKWISE FROM ABOVE:

CONTINUITY

Anonymous

This poster, bearing Bosnian coats of arms through the ages, shows that Bosnia-Herzegovina was officially recognized as member 177 of the United Nations on May 21, 1992. The type is in both Cyrillic and Latin scripts, indicating unity between Serbs, Bosnians, and Croats.

25XI BiH

Jasminko Arnautović

Tuzla, 1997

November 2, 1994, was the day Bosnia-Herzegovina was recognized as a republic within Yugoslavia. Here Arnautović makes a statement about Bosnia retaining its identity as the multiethnic state it was under Tito.

SDA—MUSLIM PARTY

Sarajevo, 1991

The year before Bosnia gained its independence and war broke out, all of the main political parties were guilty of linking politics with ethnicity and religion. Alija Izetbegović's party of Democratic Action appealed to the country's predominant Muslim electorate with a slogan not exactly designed to encourage national unity. The rest of the text reads: "They will come to negotiate about the future of our life together: Milošević, Tudjman, Kučan . . . But who will represent us? SDA—our destiny in our hands."

FOLLOWING PAGE:

BEHIND THE DREAM

Adin Šadić

Tuzla, 1995

Poster for a play at the National Theatre of Tuzla.

In the winter of 1995 Tuzla was predictably cold, wet, and smoggy from wood fires and burning rubbish. On New Year's Eve we danced in the streets amid the echo of hand grenades and automatic gunfire let off to celebrate the peacetime new year. Through it all, a ubiquitous poster with a black-and-white eye glared over the dirty town. It advertised the play *Iza Sna* ("Behind the Dream"). When I tried to acquire the poster, I found that the theater company had already run out of copies, and obtaining a clean copy became something of a mission. Three years later, in Tuzla, I met the designer Adin Šadić and mentioned this striking if somewhat inscrutable image. His face lit up: He had designed the poster, and he could give me a copy. When I asked him to explain its meaning, Šadić told me that the eye referred to the central theme of the play—the premise that Bosnia was so blinded by its love for Yugoslavia that it remained tragically unaware of the dark, nationalistic forces that were gathering within it.

The Bosnian War matters. Not just for Bosnians and people in surrounding Balkan countries, but also for the citizens of the United States, Britain, and other European nations whose governments played such a decisive role in the war. The breakup of Yugoslavia—and particularly the conflict in Bosnia—forced these nations to rethink key aspects of their foreign policy. The UN and other humanitarian organizations—all essentially funded by taxpayers—also came under close scrutiny and intense criticism. The Bosnian War, and world reaction to it, should also matter to the citizens of countless other nations that are themselves not so peaceable, or are conflicted by internal fault lines between their peoples. The posters assembled here guide the reader through the events of the Bosnian War, through the eyes of those who were actually involved in it; taken together they form a unique visual history of what took place. It is a record of which we should all be aware.

Emir Hadžihafizbegović

IZA SNA

NOTES

1. The official name of the country, in Bosnian, is Bosna i Hercegovina. Herzegovina is the southeast region. I use "Bosnia" and "Bosnia-Herzegovina" interchangeably in this text. For simplicity's sake, I also use "Yugoslavia," rather than "the former Yugoslavia," to refer to the country as it existed before the breakup.

2. For this reason I have chosen to include several images that were designed as posters but never printed.

3. There are cases of a direct relationship between Bosnian designs and well-known Polish posters. See pages 125 and 145.

4. Milošević became head of the Praesidium of the Central Committee of the League of Communists in 1986. He was elected president of the Presidency of Serbia in 1989. In 1990, after constitutional changes that led to elections in all the republics, Milošević became president of the newly formed Socialist Party of Serbia (SPS) and then president of Serbia. The SPS was little more than a renamed Communist Party. He was reelected in 1992, and then elected president of the Federal Republic of Yugoslavia in 1997. On September 24, 2000, in an early election he thought he could win, Milošević was beaten by Vojislav Koštunica. After attempting to fix the result, he was deposed on October 5. Serbia is one republic in what has been called the Federal Republic of Yugoslavia (FRY) since April 1992. In this text I often use Serbia when, technically, I should use FRY.

   President Tudjman died of cancer in December 1999. He was replaced by the relative moderate, Stjepan Mesić. Under Mesić, Croatia's previously abysmal human-rights record has begun to improve. However, according to many human-rights watchdogs, ethnic minorities in Croatia still suffer widespread discrimination.

5. The earliest and most influential nationalistic statement was a "Memorandum" penned in 1986 by sixteen leading intellectuals from the Serbian Academy of Sciences in Belgrade. The document was a tirade against non-Serbs, and warned prophetically of the imminent destruction of Serbs in Yugoslavia unless steps were taken to remedy their plight.

6. Laura Silber and Alan Little, *The Death of Yugoslavia* (London: Penguin Books/BBC Books, 1995), 37–38.

7. Milošević and four of his closest aides were indicted by the International Criminal Tribunal for the former Yugoslavia in The Hague for crimes against humanity and war crimes. The indictment, signed on May 22, 1999, was solely for crimes committed in Kosovo. At the time of this writing, Milošević has yet to be formally indicted for similar acts and much more widespread crimes committed by forces under his control in Croatia and Bosnia.

8. These autonomies were granted in 1974 under Tito. The act was seen by disgruntled Serbs as a betrayal of their interests by the half-Croat, half-Slovene leader. Although Kosovo and Vojvodina did not achieve the status of full republics, remaining constitutionally part of Serbia, they enjoyed important political, judicial, educational, and cultural rights of self-determination.

9. After the breakup of the former Yugoslavia, the Yugoslav People's Army changed its name to the Yugoslav Army, or *Vojska Jugoslavije* (VJ).

10. Karadžić was head of the Democratic Party of Serbs (Srpska Demokratska Stranka) and the so-called leader of the Bosnian Serbs. He has been indicted for war crimes by The Hague tribunal, but at the time of this writing is still free and believed to be living in the Republika Srpska, near Sarajevo.

11. Warlord, businessman, and gangster Željko "Arkan" Ražnatović was shot dead in the lobby of a Belgrade hotel in January 2000. Vojislav Šešelj is president of the ultranationalist Serb Radical Party (SRS). At the time of this writing he is still a deputy prime minister in the Serbian government. Vuk Drašković remains a leading political figure in Serbia. He was one of the earliest and most virulent exponents of a Greater Serbia, and is currently president of his parliamentary party, the Serbian Renewal Movement (SPO).

12. ABiH stands for *Armija Bosne i Hercegovine* (Army of Bosnia-Herzegovina) and is also known simply as the Bosnian Army. During the war, the ABiH was the legitimate armed force representing the elected Bosnian government, and comprised mainly, but not exclusively, Muslims. The second-in-command, Gen. Jovan Divjak, was actually a Serb. The multiethnic makeup of the ABiH was played down during the war by Serb nationalists as well as by many journalists, who thought it might confuse people.

13. Bosnia was recognized as a member of the United Nations on May 21, 1992. During the war, great efforts were made by the government in Sarajevo to have the arms embargo lifted, and indignation about it mounted around the world. Bosnia did receive small arms during the war, and rumors abound as to their often covert sources.

14. The Republika Srpska (Republic of Serbs) was officially recognized at Dayton. It constitutes 49 percent of Bosnian territory. An "interethnic boundary line" separates it from the Muslim-Croat Federation, which was forged in separate peace talks between Croatia and the Bosnian government in 1994, and constitutes the other 51 percent of the country.

15. Noel Malcolm, "Why the Peace of Paris Will Mean More War in Bosnia," *London Daily Telegraph* (December 15, 1995).

16. The HVO (which stands for Hrvatsko Vijeće Odbrane) is an essentially Herzegovinian, Croat army that, especially under Tudjman, was financially and militarily backed by Croatia proper.

   Some members of the HVO—particularly in Sarajevo and around Tuzla—continued to fight alongside the ABiH, and there was often widespread distaste among Croats outside Herzegovina for what was being done there to Muslims.

   The HVO is now an official part of Bosnia's military structure, working alongside the ABiH. The third legitimate army in Bosnia now is the Army of Bosnian Serbs, based in the Republika Srpska.

17. Serb nationalists identify many *krajinas* in the territories of the former Yugoslavia, and almost all relate to Serb military conquests achieved during previous campaigns of expansionism.

18. Anthony Borden, "The Lesson Unlearned," *War Report 58* (London: The Institute of War and Peace Reporting, 1998).

PLATES

CIAo!
Asim Delilović
Travnik, 1996

At the end of WWII, Josip Broz Tito managed to pull
Yugoslavia into a new federal state formed of six republics:
Bosnia-Herzegovina, Croatia, Macedonia, Montenegro,
Serbia, and Slovenia. Although Tito was essentially a
dictator, he was adored by most Yugoslavs and ruled for
more than 30 years. Yugoslavia under Tito was at the center
of the nonaligned movement of countries that were wholly
committed neither to the U.S. nor to the USSR. Tito died at
the age of 88 in May 1980.

Asim Delilović is the author of 27 pieces of graphic art
that were conceptualized between 1992 and 1997, although
all of them were produced after the war. Together they tell a
complete story of the war in Bosnia. This image of Tito is the
first in the series.

FOLLOWING PAGES, FROM LEFT:
SOS CROATIA
Ranko Novak
Croatia, 1991

Slovenia and Croatia declared independence from Yugoslavia
on June 25, 1991. On June 28 the JNA (Yugoslav People's
Army) invaded Slovenia. Serbia withdrew its forces after ten
days and then attacked Croatia. The ensuing war lasted four
years, although the first year was the most destructive.

In Croatian, *šah* means "chess." The red-and-white
checkerboard, called *šahovnica*, is the ancient heraldic
emblem of Croatia. Although its history dates to the Middle
Ages, during WWII it was associated with the Nazi puppet
regime that declared an independent Croatian state in
1941. This regime, headed by Ante Pavelić, murdered
hundreds of thousands of Serbs and other minorities in
Croatia in an orgy of nationalistic bloodletting. After the
defeat of the Croat fascists, Tito banned the use of the
šahovnica, and it did not appear again officially until 1990,
when newly elected president Franjo Tudjman resurrected it
in the national flag. This act, among others implemented by
Tudjman, caused great unease among Serbs living in
Croatia. In 1991 there were approximately 600,000 Serbs
living in Croatia. Today there are less than half that number.

KRVATSKA
Borislav Ljubičić
Croatia, 1991

In Croatian, *krv* means "blood" and *Hrvatska* is "Croatia." This
poster amalgamates the two words.

All the images relating to Croatia on the following nine
pages were found at the Croatian History Museum in Zagreb.
We are very grateful to the museum for allowing us to
reproduce them here.

S CROATIA S

LDS

KRVATSKA

KROATIEN
CROATIA
クロアチア
CROATIE
1 9 9 1

STOP THE WAR IN CROATIA
Ante Verzzoti
Croatia, 1991

**MY FATHER'S A CROATIAN
SOLDIER TOO**
Ivo Vrtarić
Croatia, 1992
A call-up poster for the newly formed Croatian army.

**JNA—THE TRADEMARK FOR
AGGRESSION, CRIME, MURDER**
Anonymous
1991

NO YU
Anonymous
1991
This poster was faxed anonymously to the Croatian History
Museum in Zagreb.

VUKOVAR
Anonymous
1991

DO YOU REMEMBER DUBROVNIK?
Minute
Croatia, 1991
Dubrovnik, on Croatia's Dalmatian coast, is one of the most
beautiful cities on the Adriatic. The old town is a fortress
jutting out into the sea, with white walls and tiny stone steps
winding up to the ramparts. Before the war Dubrovnik was
one of the most popular tourist attractions in Yugoslavia.

After Croatia seceded from Yugoslavia, Dubrovnik was
attacked by Montenegrin troops of the JNA from the hills
above the city. At times it seemed as if the international
community was more concerned about the damage caused
to Dubrovnik's famous old Venetian buildings than about
the fate of Croatian civilians.

STOP THE WAR
IN CROATIA

I MOJ JE
TATA
HRVATSKI
VOJNIK

ERATIVNA GRUPA »POSAVINA« – NOVSKA

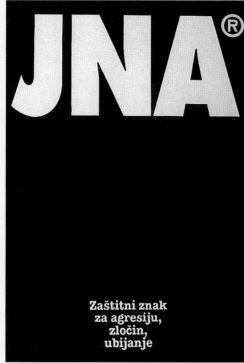

JNA®

Zaštitni znak
za agresiju,
zločin,
ubijanje

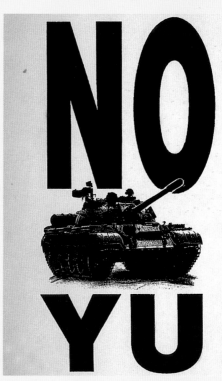

NO
YU

VUKOVAR

and the light shines in the darkness, and the darkness did not comprehend it.

SLAVONSKI BROD—WAR 1992
Mario Kučera
Croatia, 1992
This poster shows the destruction in Slavonski Brod, another Croatian town that borders Bosnia.

VUKOVAR—OUR DAILY BREAD
Anonymous
1991
While Dubrovnik was being shelled, Vukovar, a beautiful but little-known Danubian town in the east of Croatia, was leveled. Its inhabitants fled or were killed.

FOLLOWING PAGES, FROM LEFT:
TOP:
BOSNIA
Čedomir Kostović
USA, 1995
Čedomir Kostović was a leading graphic designer in Bosnia before the war. Among other things, he was part of the team responsible for the graphic design of the XIV Winter Olympics in Sarajevo in 1984. In 1991 he moved to the United States. His posters were produced with the assistance of Ken Daley at Old Dominion University in Norfolk, Virginia.

BOTTOM:
BOSNA
Asim Delilović
Travnik, 1992

STOP MILOŠEVIĆ
Began Turbić
Tuzla, 1992
In this poster an inverted hand making a traditional Serb salute is transformed into a hooded, ax-wielding killer. The eye and mouth holes of the hood form the letters SDS in Cyrillic, which stands for *Srpska Demokratska Stranka*, the Bosnian Serb political party that was supported by Slobodan Milošević and led by Radovan Karadžić.
The positioning of the fingers signifies the trinity in the Serb Orthodox church. It is also commonly used as a sign for victory by Serb soldiers, much as British and American troops use the two-fingered "V" sign. In Bosnia, it became a hated symbol of Serb military aggression.

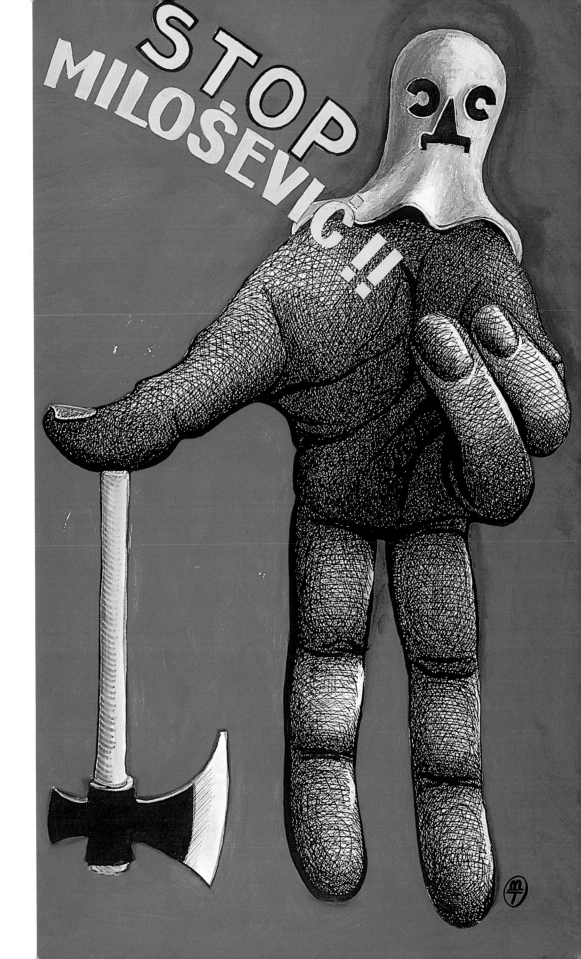

MEIN KAMPF—DOBRICA ĆOSIĆ
Began Turbić
Tuzla, 1992

The bubble in the poster reads: "This edition of the masterpiece is bound in Muslims' skin."

Dobrica Ćosić was the head of the Serbian Academy of Sciences in Belgrade. In 1986 the Academy published a now infamous document known as the "Memorandum." It is widely believed that Ćosić was responsible for writing it.

The Memorandum states that Serbs in Yugoslavia had been in a subservient position within the federation since constitutional changes made to the country under Tito in 1974, the year that Muslims were recognized as a "nationality" in Bosnia, and Kosovo and Vojvodina were made autonomous provinces. As a result, the Memorandum suggests, Serbs became the victims of genocide in Kosovo and an endangered nationality within Yugoslavia generally. The Memorandum shocked the whole of the former Yugoslavia. It presented Tito as a radical anti-Serb, and was in many ways a call to arms for the Serb nation.

Initially, it was attacked by many politicians in Serbia, including Slobodan Milošević. Later, at the height of the war in Bosnia, Milošević made Dobrica Ćosić president of the new Yugoslav Federation.

OPPOSITE:
IN ISTANBUL THE CORE, THE MYTH IS EVERMORE
Began Turbić
Tuzla, 1992

The book is titled *History, Culture, and Tradition of the Serbs.* The poster suggests that a hole will be left behind if all traces of Turkish influence are removed from Serbia.

U STAMBOLU BIT – OSTAO JE MIT

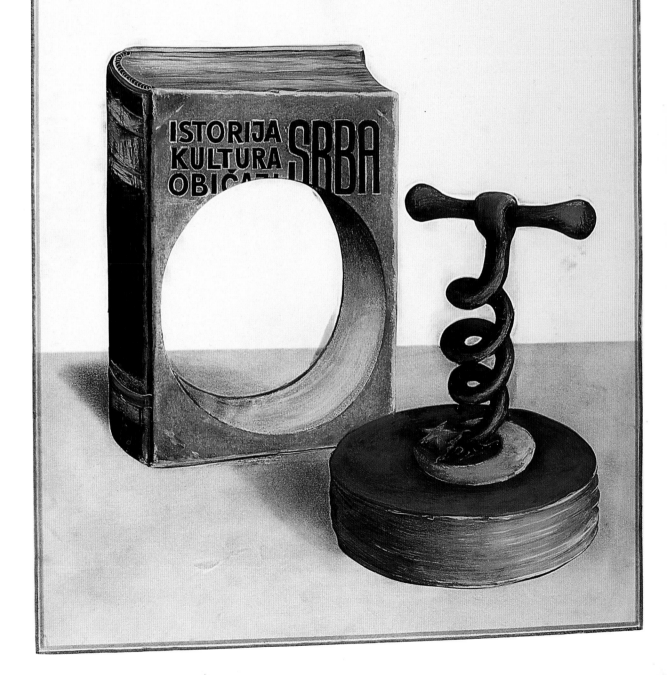

BROTHERHOOD AND UNITY
Čedomir Kostović
USA, 1994

"Brotherhood and Unity" was a popular slogan in the former Yugoslavia, used to emphasize the need for cooperation between the republics and the various nationalities. Several of the republics had fought each other during WWII, with a huge loss of life. In the years following the victory by Tito's partisans, this slogan became the unifying doctrine of the Yugoslav state.

Kostović's poster speaks of the abandonment of this concept and the brutality that was used to cut apart multiethnic Bosnia.

FOLLOWING PAGES, FROM LEFT:
DANI *Magazine Cover*
Sarajevo, February 1993

DANI (Days) magazine was launched in autumn 1992. It is privately owned and published in Sarajevo, and is probably the most unbiased news publication produced anywhere in Bosnia. It carries out in-depth investigations into subjects that most papers tend to avoid, especially if they touch on corruption or incompetence in government.

DANI covers are always stimulating and often controversial. There is a great deal of discussion among the youthful staff about their subject and style, and feelings about this can be strong. The design group TRIO has created many of the covers for the magazine, including this one.

This cover draws a comparison between Adolf Hitler and Radovan Karadžić. Karadžić was the head of the SDS (Serbian Democratic Party). He was elected to political office in the first free elections in Bosnia in November 1990. He later became a warlord, and his forces, along with Serb regulars and paramilitaries from Serbia, rampaged across the country.

Democratic Bosnians knew that Karadžić's brand of politics was nothing less than fascism disguised as nationalism. It took the rest of Europe much longer to acknowledge this, and while Bosnians were attempting to draw attention to this fact, world leaders were wining and dining Karadžić and his like.

DEATH TO TERRORISTS—MESSAGE LILIES
Ismet Hrvanović
Tuzla, 1992

Since medieval times lilies have been the symbol of Bosnia. This symbol is now more closely associated with Muslims, having been rejected by Serbs and Croats in favor of their neighboring republics' flags.

Brotherhood and Unity

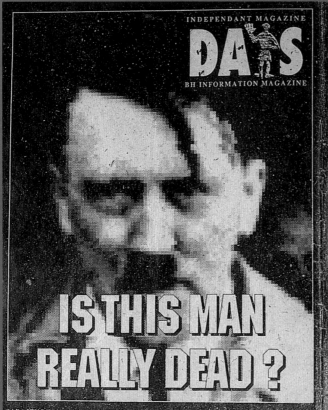

INDEPENDANT MAGAZINE

DA S
BH INFORMATION MAGAZINE

IS THIS MAN REALLY DEAD ?

SARAJEVO 5. 2. 1993. No. 8. YEAR II, PRICE 3000 BHD, 400 CRD, 200 TSL, 3 DEM, 2 USD

NEZAVISNI LIST

DAN
BH INFORMATIVNE NOVINE

DA LI JE HITLER ZAISTA MRTAV ?

SARAJEVO 5. 2. 1993. BROJ 8. GODINA II, CIJENA 3000 BHD, 400 CRD, 200 TSL, 3 DEM,

DIRECTION FREEDOM
Ismet Hrvanović
Tuzla, 1992

OPPOSITE:
SDS—JNA
Ismet Hrvanović
Tuzla, 1992
Text Translation:
TERRORISTS - AGGRESSORS
WILDERNESS - GENOCIDE
HORROR - MINDLESSNESS
KNIFE - BLOOD - DEATH
The letter "S" is *C* in the Cyrillic alphabet. The cross with four *C*s is the national Serb emblem. The abbreviation stands for *Samo Sloga Srbe Spašava*, which means "Only Unity Saves the Serbs." In this poster, the emblem is transformed into four snakes within an egg.

**TERORISTI·AGRESORI
PUSTOŠ·GENOCID·UŽAS
BEZUMLJE·NOŽ·KRV·SMR**

AGGRESSION AGAINST BOSNIA-HERZEGOVINA
TRIO
Sarajevo, 1992

OPPOSITE:
AGGRESSION AGAINST BOSNIA-HERZEGOVINA
TRIO
Sarajevo, 1992

FOLLOWING PAGES, FROM LEFT:
I AM TO—AND YOU?
Zdravko Novak
Tuzla, 1992
TO stands for *Teritorialna Odbrana*, meaning "Territorial
Defense." *To* also means "it," giving the title a double
meaning. In the former Yugoslavia each republic had its
own TO. These forces were made up of civilians who could
be mobilized at short notice in the event of invasion by
foreign powers.

On April 4, 1992, Bosnian President Alija Izetbegović
mobilized the Bosnian TO following attacks by the JNA and
Serb paramilitaries. Though Radovan Karadžić claimed that
Izetbegović's mobilization constituted a declaration of war
against Bosnia's Serbs, the war had in reality already been
declared by Milošević.

This poster was produced in Tuzla at the end of 1992,
when there was an emphasis on creating propaganda
material aimed at encouraging men to enlist. Three
thousand copies of the poster were printed and posted, but
few remain. We found this one in the Army Museum in
Tuzla.

WE ARE TO
TO
Sarajevo, 1992

AGRESIJA NA BOSNU I HERCEGOVINU

REPUBLIKA BOSNA I HERCEGOVINA

AGRESIJA
NA BOSNU I
HERCEGOVINU

REPUBLIKA BOSNA I HERCEGOVINA

TO SMO MI!

TO-BIH

TOP LEFT:
GENERAL MOBILIZATION
Anonymous
Bijeljina, 1992
The words on this Bosnian Serb call-up poster read, "General Mobilization for All—ABSOLUTELY ALL—Men Aged Between 18 and 60."

The Bosnian Serb Army was created in the first few months of the war. It was heavily supplemented with arms and men from the JNA and Serb paramilitaries.

TOP RIGHT:
BOSNIAN SERB ARMY CALENDAR
Anonymous
Bijeljina, 1994
A local Rambo look-alike from Bijeljina.

BOTTOM LEFT:
PATRIOTIC LEAGUE—1ST ANNIVERSARY
Fuad Kasumović
Tuzla, 1992
The Patriotic League was the armed wing of the Muslim-dominated SDA (Party of Democratic Action), the ruling party in Bosnia-Herzegovina. In 1992 the Army of Bosnia-Herzegovina (ABiH) was created out of the Territorial Defense and the Patriotic League.

BOTTOM RIGHT:
PATRIOTIC LEAGUE—4TH ANNIVERSARY
Fuad Kasumović
Tuzla, 1995

ОПШТА
МОБИЛИЗАЦИЈА
ЗА СВЕ,
АПСОЛУТНО СВЕ
МУШКАРЦЕ ОД 18 ДО 60 ГОДИНА

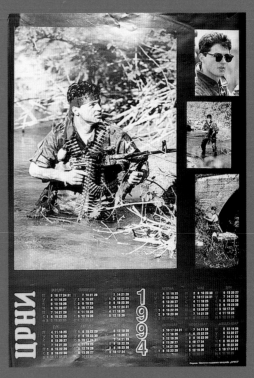

ЦРНИ 1994

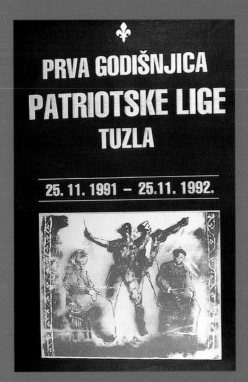

PRVA GODIŠNJICA
PATRIOTSKE LIGE
TUZLA

25. 11. 1991 – 25. 11. 1992.

PATRIOTSKA LIGA
TUZLA

P.L. BiH

Dani patriotske lige

25.11.91.

25.11.91. – 25.11.95.

OUR FATHER'S IN THE HVO TOO—AND YOURS?
Art Forces
Mostar, 1993
A call-up poster from early 1993 for the HVO in
Herzegovina (southwestern Bosnia). HVO stands for *Hrvatsko
Vijeće Odbrane* ("Croatian Defense Council"). It was formed
in early 1992 to counter the Serb offensive in Herzegovina,
but was later used to attack Muslims in Bosnia.

FOLLOWING PAGES:
LEFT PAGE:
THE FATE OF BiH IS IN OUR HANDS—JOIN US!
Bato Bato
Tuzla, 1992

RIGHT PAGE:
TOP LEFT:
JOIN US
E. Husanović and D. Srabović
Tuzla, 1993

TOP RIGHT:
BOSNIA DEFENDS ITSELF ON THE DRINA
Nijaz Omerović
Gračanica, 1994
Historically, the Drina River formed the natural border
separating western Serbia and eastern Bosnia.

BOTTOM:
WE ARE IN THE ARMY OF BiH—WHAT ABOUT YOU?
Nijaz Omerović
Gračanica, 1992

i naš je tata u
HVO, a
tvoj?

armija republike bosne i hercegovine

Borac

deSign by bato bato & caop 5.og tuzla

SUDBINA BiH JE U NAŠIM RUKAMA
PRIDRUŽITE NAM SE !

pp FIBBOS - braća Azapagić   štampa / ratna štamparija 2.korpusa

PRIDRUŽITE NAM SE

SPONZOR: Izdavačko prometno preduzeće R&R Tuzla   DESIGN: E.Husanović & D.Srabović   TUZLA 1993

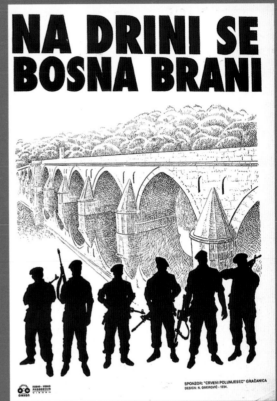

NA DRINI SE BOSNA BRANI

SPONZOR: "CRVENI POLUMJESEC" GRAČANICA
DESIGN: N. OMEROVIĆ - 1994.

MI SMO U ARMIJI BIH
A VI

Sponzor "SPEKTRA" Gračanica
Design: H. Omerović

TOGETHER
Adin Šadić
Tuzla, 1992

Šadić, a Bosnian Muslim fighter in the Tuzla region, produced this image in 1992. He was a member of the Black Swans, an elite fighting force made up of Croats and Muslims. Šadić drew this picture before the Croat-Muslim split, which led to a tripartite war in Bosnia between Serbs, Croats, and Muslims. The red-and-white helmet in the colors of the Croatian flag signifies Bosnia's Croats. Bosnia is represented by the blue-and-white fleurs-de-lis.

At the beginning of the war there was genuine optimism that Serb expansionism in Bosnia could be defeated through the combined efforts of Bosnia's Croats and Muslims. In Herzegovina and central Bosnia, however, this hope was short-lived. In 1993, Franjo Tudjman, the president of Croatia, decided to annex Herzegovina and the HVO was ordered to attack its Muslim allies.

ZAJEDNO

ART WORK · AOV4 '92.

TOP:

URBICIDE—MOSTAR '92
Željko Schnatinger
Vladimir Kolapić, photographer
Mostar, 1992
Long before the Croats attacked east Mostar, the Serbs had shelled the city from the hills. This poster was one of a series drawing attention to the material damage created during 1992.

BOTTOM:

URBICIDE '92
Alija Hafizović Haf and Vanja Fundić Hafizović
Sarajevo, 1992
The term "urbicide" was coined during the recent wars in the Balkans as a way of describing the deliberate destruction of cities. Countless towns and cities were devastated by Serb as well as Croat forces in an attempt to displace civilians and destroy their history and culture.

OPPOSITE:

UNTITLED
Kemal Hadžić, photographer
Sarajevo, 1993
On August 25, 1992, Serb forces besieging Sarajevo fired an incendiary shell into the National and University Library. It took two days to burn. Most of the library's literature was destroyed, including thousands of irreplaceable Ottoman treasures. Libraries and historic and cultural sites were targeted during the war as part of a deliberate attempt to destroy Bosnia's Islamic heritage.

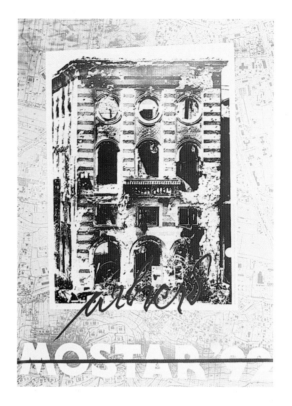

festival sarajevo

sarajevska zima '93   sarajevo winter '93

ABOVE LEFT:
**ONE AND ONLY ONE IS POSSIBLE—
A FREE BOSNIA-HERZEGOVINA**
Alija Hafizović Haf
Sarajevo, 1992

ABOVE RIGHT:
DEATH TO FASCISM—FREEDOM TO THE PEOPLE
Alija Hafizović Haf
Sarajevo, 1992
The title of this poster is adapted from a Communist slogan
that was well known to the people of the former Yugoslavia.

OPPOSITE:
UNTITLED
Enis Selimović
Sarajevo, 1993
This famous poster was photographed in the destroyed
National and University Library, where concerts were often
held before the war. The cellist Vedran Smajlović is a
legendary figure in Sarajevo. He defied all odds by staging
open-air concerts in Sarajevo at the height of the conflict.

festival sarajevo
sarajevska zima '93 ✳ sarajevo winter '93

HELP
Began Turbić
Tuzla, 1992

OPPOSITE:
SHOO CHICKEN HERDERS!
TO
Sarajevo, 1992
Led by Mirko Jović, the White Eagles were one of many
ragtag Serbian paramilitaries operating in Bosnia. They
were linked to the Belgrade-based Serbian Popular Renewal
party (SNO), and had a fierce reputation.

   In 1992 the White Eagles attacked Sarajevo, and were
defeated for the first time in their short but violent history. A
journalist asked a member of the Bosnian Special Forces
how they had managed to defeat this supposedly invincible
unit. His reply: "What eagles! These are just common
chickens!" The shape of the chicken's body and Bosnia
are roughly the same.

ARMY OF BiH
Srdanović
Zenica, 1993

In this poster, a soldier from the ABiH touches the hand imprint on a *stečak*. These medieval tombstones, which can be found at various sites in Bosnia, demonstrate Bosnia's independent existence as a country before it was colonized by successive foreign empires. The shield that appears on the arm of the soldier is the old emblem of Bosnia, which was readopted in 1992 by the newly independent state. It was, however, rejected by Serbs as well as Croats in those areas of Bosnia they controlled, as each sought to secede from Bosnia-Herzegovina. Both communities took their emblems from the neighboring republics with which they were aligned.

In 1998 the international community designed a new Bosnian flag, which has not been received with enthusiasm in any camp.

ARMIJA B.H

MOGU NAM KUĆU SRUŠITI, ALI SRCE NE!

(Riječi branioca Sarajeva sa Širokače)

TO BIH

ABOVE:
THEY CAN DESTROY OUR HOMES BUT
NOT OUR HEARTS!
TO
Sarajevo, 1992

OPPOSITE:
WE WILL WIN
TO
Sarajevo, 1992

REPUBLIKA BOSNA I HERCEGOVINA

pobijedićemo

TO-BIH

ENJOY SARAJEVO
TRIO
Sarajevo, 1992–93
TRIO is run by Bojan and Dada Hadžihalilović, a Sarajevo-based husband-and-wife team who have produced a series of now internationally famous images. The Hadžihalilovićs partnered with Lejla Mulabegović in 1985.

TRIO's most renowned images are a series of 40 postcards, all redesigns of well-known images. One of the most famous used the Coca-Cola logo.

TRIO used the postcard format for a number of reasons. At the time of their production, Sarajevo had been under siege for over a year and a half, and there was little paper or ink in the city. TRIO also wanted a product that could be sent out of the city easily, in order to communicate with as many people as possible in the outside world.

This particular poster was, ironically, printed on an old JNA (Yugoslav People's Army) map because of chronic paper shortages.

WELCOME TO SARAJEVO
Asim Delilović
Travnik, 1992

Enjoy Sarajevo 1992/93

Coca-Cola logo - redesigned by "Trio" - Sarajevo

Welcome to Sarajevo

FAMA MAP
Suada Kapić
Sarajevo, 1996

Many thousands of copies of this map have now been sold, and it has been distributed around the world. It is even displayed in the offices of the International Criminal Tribunal for the former Yugoslavia in The Hague.

Sarajevo was attacked on April 5, 1992, and by May 2 was totally blockaded. The city was surrounded by more than 250 tanks and 100 mortars, as well as antiaircraft guns and snipers. The siege lasted until February 26, 1996, making it the longest in modern times: 1,395 days.

On the back of the map FAMA states that altogether 10,615 people were killed in Sarajevo, including 1,601 children. More than 50,000 were wounded.

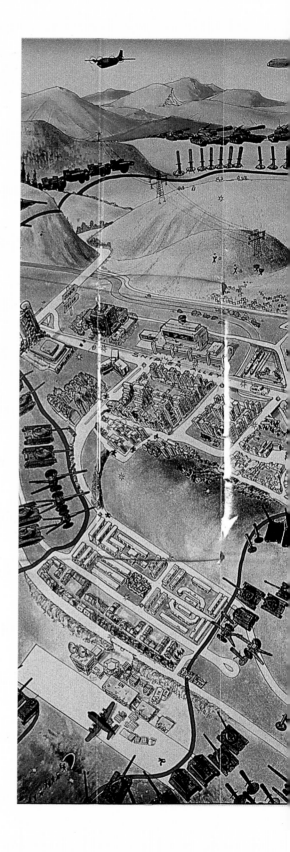

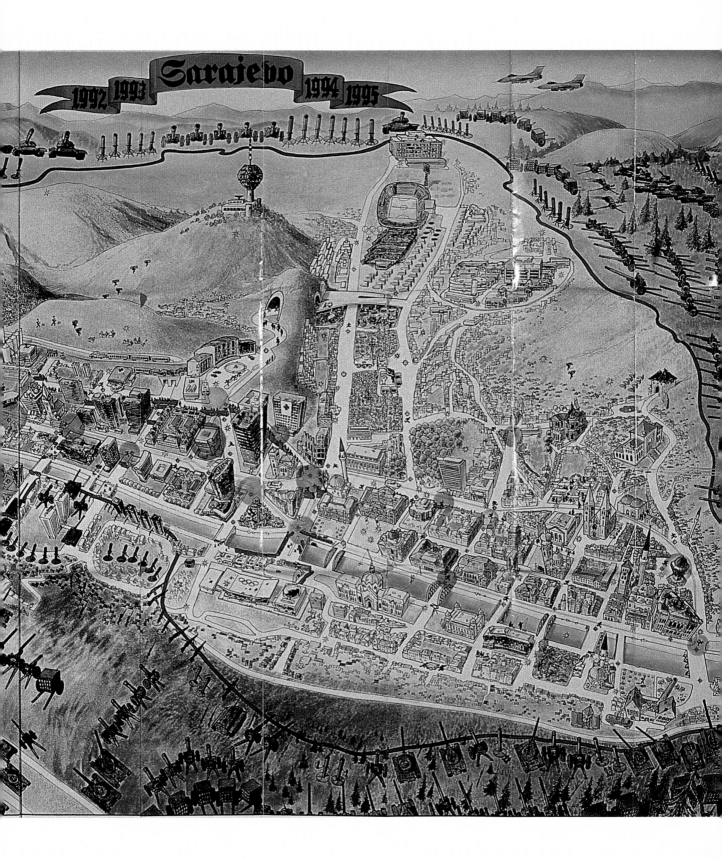

SARAJEVO 92 93 9?
Čedomir Kostović
USA, 1993

SARAJEVO
92 93 9 ?
years of dangerous living

PERFECT
Asim Delilović
Travnik, 1992

This poster was inspired by the death of Suada Deliberović, a 21-year-old medical student, on a bridge in Sarajevo on April 6, 1992. Deliberović, who was shot by a sniper during a peace demonstration, was the first person to die violently in Sarajevo, and her death shocked those in Bosnia who had not believed that full-scale war was possible. Today, the bridge bears her name.

The sniper in this poster wears glasses, symbolizing the involvement of Serb intellectuals in the destruction of Bosnia-Herzegovina. The translation of his thought is "Perfect."

LEO NEWS
Malik "Kula" Kulenović
Sarajevo, 1993–94

Kula is a legendary figure in Sarajevo. He never left the city
during the siege, and produced his own handwritten news
bulletins throughout, which were posted in a sheltered
street where he sold other newspapers. His "paper" was
called *Leo News*, and each daily edition was numbered with
the day of the siege. *Leo News* was written in a combination
of Cyrillic and Latin scripts to signify ethnic unity. As such,
quite apart from its content, it made a powerful political
statement. Because of its colloquial use of language, precise
translation is impossible.

OPPOSITE, TOP ROW:
DAY 337/425
Sarajevo, 1993

OPPOSITE, BOTTOM ROW:
DAY 613/672
Sarajevo, 1993–94

FOLLOWING PAGES, FROM LEFT:
DAY 531/308
Sarajevo, 1993

QUESTIONNAIRE III
1993

Kula posted a number of questionnaires. This one asks:
Why did we fight?
For freedom?
For an independent BiH?
For a business office?
For a country of three nations?

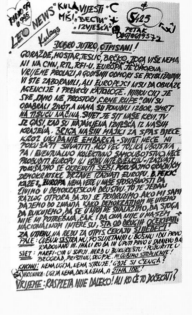

"LEO NEWS" Kula93 — "VIJESTI" "BECTU" "IZVJEŠĆA"

RADIO 99! "925." — 531 — SUBOTA 18/09/93

DOBRO JUTRO, EUROPO!

ŽESTOK RITAM JUTRA, RATNOG SARAJEVA, SLUŠAM RADIO.
MUZIKA SKETNOG VREMENA. MUZIKA OPTIMIZMA I DRAGA IMENA:
HAMO, RADENKO, FUDO, ZOKA, MESTAR I SARMER FAZLA...
HOR, GLASOVI MLADOSTI, GLASOVI AMELE, ANELE, JELENE, ISPUNJAVAJU
SOBIČAK I KROZ OTVOREN PROZOR, ŠIRE SE GRADOM. SREĆA JE
ŽIV STIĆI DO PRVE LINIJE. SREĆA JE OTVORITI KONZERVU.
SREĆA JE PISMO SINA, DOBITI. LUDILO JE ČUTI: -TATA, JE'L JOŠ KOJI
PEDERSKI METAK U SOBU, UŠO? !- JESU LI GELERI SLJIVU, OTRESLI?
VALOVI I MUZIKA, UZBUĐUJU ME. DIŠEM. GUTAM ZRAK. ŠIRIM
RUKE. HUMI MJE BOGZNA KAKVA. ZADNJA KONZERVA, ZELENA
MASNIH SLOVA - POKLON TALIJANSKE VLADE! - DONO DEL GOVERNO
ITALIANO!, PUKLA JE SINOĆ UZ UNMER LUK I PIVO MALO-SARAJEVSKO.
ROK UPOTREBE KONZERVE DAVNO JE PROSAO. ROK UNIŠTENJA GRADA
NJEGOVOG DUHA, MLADOSTI, ZNANJA JE GOSPODO EUROPEJCI-ISTERAO
VAŠE OGLEDALO I VAŠ JUTARNJI LIK U NJEMU NIKAD NEĆE BITI TAKO
LIJEPO, KAO ŠTO JE TO DANAS PROBUĐENI STANOVNIK SARAJEVA.
NI SLOMLJENO OGLEDALO, NE MOŽE SAKRITI LJEPOTU NJEGOVIH LICA,
SJAJ U OČIMA.
DANAS SLAVIMO, DANAS JE OPET EUROPA TU I MI U NJOJ.
DANAS SMO PONOVO NA VALOVIMA RADIO 99.

(IZ DNEVNIKA SLUŠAOCA NA ČEKANJU)

KRONIKA UŽASA

ZAGREB: -IZVJEŠTAJ SA SLUŽBENOG PUTA-PRIHVAĆEN. RIZNICA PERA
JA POTPISA PRIMIRJA, DEKLARACIJA-BOGATIJA ZA DVA PERA.
- ŠKOLSKA GODINA JE DUGA, A PERA SE TROŠE!
MOSTAR: -OVO ODUŠEVLJENO POZDRAVIO, POTPISIVANJE-GRANATAMA!
MOSTARCE DUŠE I DANAS OTIŠLE U NEBO!
PALE: -PALEOLITI DVE LINIJE RAZGRANIČENJA UVRDILI PRIMIRJE.
-GRANATAMA I SILAČIMA STAVLJEN JE POTPIS SVJEDOKA.
BIHAĆ: AUTONOMAŠI BEZ REFERENDUMA.
BANJA LUKA: UHVAĆEN ZEC I RADOVAN RUČALO U BOSNI.
KOSTI POKUPILI BOJOVNICI PRAVOSLAVLJA "I ODNIJELI NA MANJAČU
EEZ: PARLAMENT GLASAO ZA VOJNU INTERVENCIJU! HAHAA!
SA HRONIKA: -U GRADU SU SAFARI-MENOVI! ČUVAJTE SE!
-USKORO OKLOPNI VLAK ZA ZENICU!
-NA SKENDERIJI-DVA PRVAKA U MILJACKI!
NAKON BURNE NOĆI-BILO JE TO PRANJE SAVJESTI!
-TKO NE ZNA TENIS IGRATI-MOŽE DA UDI UZ "TENIS 2."
-KONVOJI ZA 15 DANA-INŠALAH!!

(PAZI NA HLOR!)

VRIJEME: JE POTPISA-IDITE MATIČARU!

LEO NEWS Kula93 — VIJESTI BECTU IZVJEŠĆA

308 — PETAK 29/01/93

DANAS JE 290-ti DAN,
KAKO JE OVAJ MALI GRAĐANIN
SARAJEVA, OTIŠAO U
EUROPU.

OTIŠAO JE, A U PISMU PIŠE:

"STALNO MISLIM NA TEBE,
DRAGI MOJ TATA, NA MOJE
SARAJEVO I NA MOJU BiH."

NE OKREĆI SE SINE!

SA HRONIKA: NA KONFERENCIJI ZA TISAK I RTV,
VRLI NAM G. HAMO PORUČUJE:

"SABUR - SELAMET" *

EKSKLUZIVNO

* VIDI A. ŠKALJIĆ-TURCIZMI U SJ STR 539
- "U VELJAČI BIT ĆE I SOMUNA"

"L.N." BUDITE PAŽLJIVI: TO NIJE
LED, NIJE NI SNIJEG. OVO SU
"DUŠE" STANOVNIKA SARAJEVA.

-IZ VIK'a: OSTAVI PREDU, Mr. GURDA,
FAĆAJ SE METLE I ČISTI SVOJU
AVLIJU.

-IRFO: "NEŠ' TI MENI PREDLI,
HAMO, PREDO & AJ, FURAMO
NA EUROVIZIJU '93."

"L.N": ŠTA JE SA JOKINOM RAJOM?

"LEO NEWS"
kula93

ANKETA - BR.3.
UPIŠITE!

a) ZA SLOBODU...

b) ZA JEDINSTVENU BH-A...

c) ZA POSLOVNI PROSTOR...

d) ZA DRŽAVU TRI DRŽAVE...

ZAŠTO SMO
SE BORILI?

VETERANI

ZA DANE RADOSTI

— ZA KANISTER S VAŽEĆIM
AKUMULATOR I KONZERVU
BEZ KRMETINE!
P.S. DA ODEM NA MORE!
DA POSTANEM PILOT I DA OTKAČIN GAJDE OD LJUDI
• PER ESSERE LIBERI DI RITROVARCI INSIEME SOTTO UN CIELO STELLATO

— Da se odselim od mene !!!

— Da što prije odem odavde

— Za definitivni dokaz da su Mravojedi najljepši i da kao takvi trebaju ići pa-pa

— Za

— ZA POSLOVNI PROSTOR IŠTAN INISTO OCADA

— DA NEMAMO STRUJE!

— Ct ČUVANJE ŽENSKI OTOECO 17-24 GODINE

ABOVE LEFT:
IT'S NOT IMPORTANT TO WIN—BUT TO SURVIVE
Enis Selimović
Sarajevo, 1995
Baron de Coubertin, founder of the modern Olympics,
stated that "the important thing in the Olympic Games is
not winning, but taking part." TRIO turned this slogan on its
head in one of its postcards, and here Enis Selimović
entirely reinterprets it. The figure in this unpublished poster
grasps another of TRIO's postcards, *Sarajevo Summer 1992*.

ABOVE RIGHT:
DO YOU REMEMBER SARAJEVO?
TRIO
Sarajevo, 1992

TRIO studios produced a series of posters bearing this
slogan. Vučko the Wolf was the official mascot of the XIV
Sarajevo Winter Olympics in 1984, and a much-loved
symbol of the city.

OPPOSITE:
1984 SARAJEVO 1994
TRIO
Sarajevo, 1994
This postcard marks the tenth anniversary of the Winter
Olympic Games. Two years before this card was produced
Sarajevo's Olympic Museum was hit by incendiary shells
and burned to the ground along with all its artifacts.

1984 SARAJEVO 1994

Design "Trio" Sarajevo

OPPOSITE:

TOP LEFT:

UNTITLED
Began Turbić
Tuzla, 1992

Bosnia is depicted here as a bull in a bullfight, pierced by two knives—one Serbian, the other Croatian—and stuck by the lances of the international community.

TOP RIGHT:

UN—BAD MANDATE AND GOOD APPETITE
Began Turbić
Tuzla, 1992

In this unpublished poster, the double-headed eagle of Serbia is perched atop a crumbling UN. During the war, the popular sentiment in Bosnia was that the policies of the United Nations actually favored the aggressors rather than those under attack.

BOTTOM LEFT:

UN—WHO SAYS THEY'RE NOT MOVING A FINGER FOR BiH
Began Turbić
Tuzla, 1992

Turbić singles out the British and French for special ridicule in their handling of the Bosnian crisis. Although the poster presented the subject in a humorous light, the accusations were real. Led by Prime Minister John Major, Britain blocked attempts to lift the arms embargo against Bosnia-Herzegovina. France, under President François Mitterand, appeared to heavily support Serb nationalists.

BOTTOM RIGHT:

WE ARE PRISONERS OF THE UN
Began Turbić
Tuzla, *1992*

Here civilians are bound by the UN's impotence in dealing with those responsible for the war. The UN aid program, represented by the falling loaf of bread, was criticized as a substitute for political will and action.

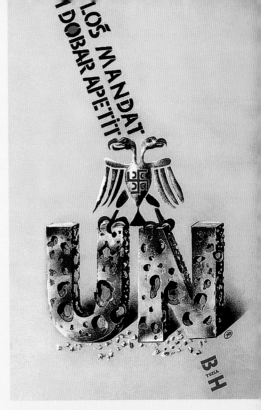

LOŠ MANDAT
DOBAR APETIT

KO KAŽE DA
NE MRDAJU
NI PRSTOM
ZA BOSNU I
HERCEGOVINU

MI SMO
ZATOČENICI
UN-a

OMARSKA—NAME OF THE ROSES IN BOSNIA
Art Publishing
Sarajevo, 1994

The concentration camp at Omarska was located in an abandoned mining complex, in what is now the Republika Srpska. This poster features the floor plan of the Omarska buildings and takes its title from Umberto Eco's *The Name of the Rose*, a novel about a series of murders in a labyrinthine medieval monastery.

Among the many buildings at Omarska were the "White House," where severe beatings were administered, and the "Red House," from which few prisoners emerged alive. The camp was surrounded by three rings of guards; only two people are known to have escaped.

At Omarska prisoners were separated into categories. "Category A" prisoners consisted of intellectuals and Muslim community and religious leaders, as well as volunteers in any of the Muslim militias or the Territorial Defense. These prisoners were generally executed immediately after their arrival.

DANI *Magazine Cover*
Sarajevo, January 1995

This cover contrasts two pictures of concentration camps, one from WWII, the other from Bosnia. The slogan on the left reads "The Camps Remain"; the one on the right says "Everything Passes."

WAR CRIMINAL—RADOVAN KARADŽIĆ
TRIO
Sarajevo, 1992

The poster reads:

Radovan Karadžić, president of the terrorist Serb Democratic Party. Born: 19.6.1945. Place of birth: Savnik, Socialist Republic of Yugoslavia. Occupation: neuropsychologist.

He is directly responsible for arming and training members of the SDS with the aim of capturing territory of the Republic of Bosnia-Herzegovina and declaring a mono-national Serb Republic in Bosnia-Herzegovina. He organized the movement of Arkan's men, Šešelj's White Eagles, and the royalists, as well as other paid criminals from Serbia and Montenegro, with the aim of ethnically cleansing territories. He ordered the attacks on Bijeljina, Foča, Sarajevo, Široki Brijeg, Odžac, Višegrad, and many other towns. He ordered the blockade of unconquered towns in order to starve the population, and attacked them with artillery and snipers. He ordered the opening of camps for the Muslim and Croat populations. He has been responsible for the deaths of 127,448 people, the wounding of 129,000 people, the displacement of 700,000 people from their homes within BiH, and the expulsion of 800,000 people from the republic.

This is all in line with his announcement that a whole nation would "disappear from the face of the earth." He is responsible for starting the war in BiH, mass-murder, rape, torture, humiliation, and genocide—acts that, under international law, fall into the category of war crimes. He will also be responsible before his own people, as he led them into crime.

WAR CRIMINAL—RATKO MLADIĆ
TRIO
Sarajevo, 1992

The accusations against Mladić, the commanding general of the Bosnian Serb Army, are in English. Both posters were produced and displayed just a few months after the Bosnian War began and a full three years before the International Tribunal in The Hague officially indicted Mladić and Karadžić.

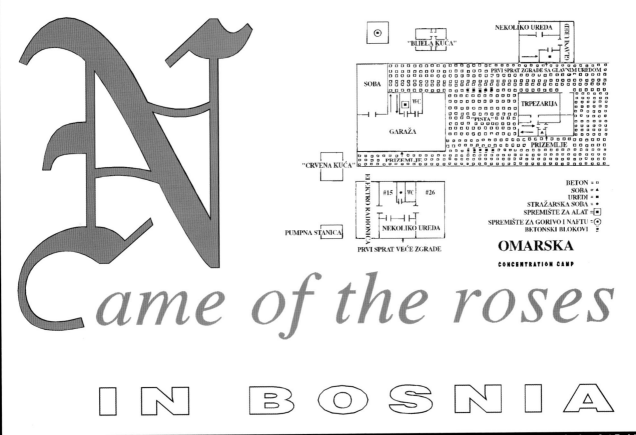

N̶ame of the roses

IN BOSNIA

design Art Publishing

KOMISIJI ZA ISTRAŽIVANJE RATNIH ZLOČINA U BOSNI I HERCEGOVINI
RATNI ZLOČINAC
TO THE COMMISION FOR THE INVESTIGATION OF THE WAR CRIMINALS IN BOSNIA AND HERZEGOVINA
WAR CRIMINAL

RADOVAN KARADŽIĆ, predsjednik terorističke Srpske demokratske stranke.
Rođen 19. 6. 1945. Mjesto rođenja Šavnik, SR Jugoslavija. Zanimanje - neuropsihijatar.
Direktno odgovoran za organizovano naoružavanje i obuku članova SDS-a s ciljem zauzimanja teritorija RBiH i proglašenje jednonacionalne tzv. Srpske Republike BiH. Pripremao dovođenje arkanovaca, šešeljevaca, Belih orlova, rojalista i drugih plaćenih kriminalaca iz Srbije i Crne Gore s ciljem provođenja etničkog čišćenja teritorija. Naredio da se napadnu Bijeljina, Foča, Sarajevo, Široki Brijeg, Očžak, Višegrad i mnogi drugi gradovi. Naredio da se neosvojena mjesta blokiraju radi izgladnjivanja stanovništva i izvrgnu artiljerijskim napadima kao i djelovanju snjaperista. Naredio otvaranje logora za muslimansko i hrvatsko stanovništvo. Do sada odgovoran za smrt 127.448, ranjavanje 129.000 lica, za progon sa svojih ognjišta 700.000 lica unutar BiH i preko 800.000 van granica BiH, što je u skladu sa njegovom najavom o nestanku sa lica zemlje, "cijelog jednog naroda". Odgovaraće za početak rata u BiH, masovna ubistva, silovanja, mučenja, poniživanja, genocid - djela koja su u međunarodnom pravu svrstana u ratne zločine. Odgovaraće i pred sopstvenim narodom jer ga je poveo u zločin.

KOMISIJI ZA ISTRAŽIVANJE RATNIH ZLOČINA U BOSNI I HERCEGOVINI

RATNI ZLOČINAC

TO THE COMMISION FOR THE INVESTIGATION OF THE WAR CRIMINALS IN BOSNIA AND HERZEGOVINA

WAR CRIMINAL

RATKO MLADIĆ, a JNA officer, the ex-commander of the 2nd Military Region with the Headquarters in Sarajevo. He carried out armament of the SDS by all kinds of weapons from the magazines of the ex-JNA. He trained the SDS extremists in handling the armament of the ex-JNA in the military grounds. He ordered the concentration of Serbian terrorist units around Sarajevo and other towns, on which he planned the attacks. He ordered the acctive assistance of JNA units to chetniks in their attacks on inhabited places. Together with a group of officers he ordered the attack on Sarajevo, on April, 6th, 1992. He directed missiles, both to the selected buildings of industrial, cultural, historical and humanitarian inportance and to the civilians. He had previously, organized and placed groups of snipers. He ordered setting fire to more significant buildings and then the use of the artillery in order to prevent the extingushing fires. He ordered the firing of places, where citizens gatnered in order to buy food. He is respondible for the death and permanent disability of thousansds of people. Due to the use of forbidden methods of war waging, defined by the Geneve Convetion from 1949, he will be convicted as a war criminal.

TRNOPOLJE
Asim Delilović
Travnik, 1993
Trnopolje was a Serb-run transit camp that held prisoners who had survived the death camps and were waiting to be exchanged for Serb prisoners. The conditions at Trnopolje were as grim, however, as those at Omarska and other camps. Detainees were routinely mistreated, tortured, and killed.

TR**NO**POLJE

TOP:
19641994—TUZLA PORTRAIT GALLERY—30 YEARS
Edin Derviševič
Tuzla, 1994

BOTTOM:
4 APRIL '92
Jasminko Arnautović
Tuzla, 1992

The town symbol of Tuzla, a large industrial and mining town in the northeast of Bosnia, is a goat. During the Austro-Hungarian occupation, goats were forbidden on the grounds that they indiscriminately ate the forests. Legend has it that there was only one goat in Tuzla, but that people still had plenty of cheese and milk—the parable being an illustration of the town's resistance to external interference.

April 4, 1992 was the day President Alija Izetbegović mobilized the Territorial Defense forces.

OPPOSITE:
EVIL DOESN'T LIVE HERE
Edin Derviševič
Tuzla, 1992

The history of opposition to nationalism in Tuzla, where Derviševič lives and works, dates to WWII. Then, as now, the citizens of Tuzla stood for the right of all to coexist peacefully.

In the recent war, Tuzla's ideals were vociferously championed by Mayor Selim Bešlagić, who earned international fame for his efforts to hold Tuzla's ethnic mix together. Tuzla is unique in that it has never fallen under the control of any one nationalist party.

ZLO NE STANUJE OVDJE

E.DERVIŠEVIĆ & D.KAPIDŽIĆ

tuzlanska banka d.d. tuzla

15 MAY '92
Jasminko Arnautović
Tuzla, 1992

On May 15, 1992, JNA soldiers attempted to leave their garrison near the center of Tuzla with their weapons. Their plan was to encircle the town before shelling it into submission, as they had done throughout Bosnia. Unlike many other towns, however, Tuzla had prepared for likely Serb aggression and there were snipers placed on high buildings along the JNA's route. The JNA opened fire before they left town, but the snipers managed to pick off drivers in the leading trucks, blocking the convoy's forward movement. Before long the entire convoy was in flames. This was the JNA's first defeat in Bosnia, and it undoubtedly saved Tuzla from being ethnically cleansed and occupied by the Serbs.

9 MAY—VICTORY OVER FASCISM DAY?
Jasminko Arnautović
Tuzla, 1992

The ninth of May is celebrated in many European countries as the day fascism was defeated. It was the day, in 1945, when the Allies entered Berlin.

Here Jasminko Arnautović juxtaposes the European Community flag with a scene from *Guernica*, Pablo Picasso's 1937 painting of the tragic Spanish Civil War bombardment.

NOTE:

The following eight posters were produced in early 1993 at the request of the Ministry of Information of the Republika Srpska. They were printed and distributed in a campaign that aimed to gain international public sympathy for the Serb cause. According to Draško Mikanović, one of the designers who contributed to the series, "The posters don't really reflect our opinion of what happened here during the war. They are just poor attempts to say the things that were not presented to the world in the way they should have been." Mikanović claims these are the only propaganda posters the Bosnian Serbs produced during the war, and that although he did not initially want to design them, he felt he had to. "We were blown away with the Croatian propaganda, and some coming from the Muslim side," he said.

The posters were drawn with gouache, and each was printed in an edition of 500 copies. There was a plan to continue producing them, but the designers were disgusted when they were sold at a profit instead of being distributed for free to Serbian communities abroad. According to Mikanović, this resulted in the Serbs losing the Bosnian propaganda war.

Three designers who collaborated with Mikanović on these posters asked not to be credited.

OPPOSITE:
TOP LEFT:
YOU'LL LISTEN TO THE SNAKE—EVE DID THE SAME
Draško Mikanović et al.
Banja Luka, 1993
All three posters on this page express anti-Croat themes.

TOP RIGHT:
THE BEAST IS OUT AGAIN
Draško Mikanović et al.
Banja Luka, 1993
This poster links together present-day Croatia, under Franjo Tudjman, with the fascist Independent State of Croatia, led by Ante Pavelić during World War II. Pavelić's Croatia was allied with Nazi Germany from 1941 to 1945, and committed genocide against hundreds of thousands of Serbs and other minorities.

Tudjman's election as president of the first independent Croatian state since 1945 spread fear among Serbs in Croatia. This was exploited by the regime in Belgrade in order to annex Serb-populated areas of Croatia. Eventually some 300,000 of Croatia's Serbs were made homeless and stateless.

BOTTOM:
NASTY KID OF A NASTY MOTHER
Draško Mikanović et al.
Banja Luka, 1993
Here Croatia is the "kid," Germany the "mother."

FOLLOWING PAGES, FROM LEFT:
YOU CAN PREVENT THIS
Draško Mikanović et al.
Banja Luka, 1993
An American war widow receives the Stars and Stripes. Both posters on this page were meant as a warning to the international community.

WHY DON'T YOU COME IN PEACE?
Draško Mikanović et al.
Banja Luka, 1993

THIS IS NOT A PAINT COMMERCIAL—THIS IS FUTURE
Draško Mikanović et al.
Banja Luka, 1993
The color green is identified with Islam. This poster implies that the whole of Europe is in danger of being Islamicized, starting with Bosnia. Through their history, Serbs often saw themselves as the defenders of Christian Europe against the Islamic hordes from the East.

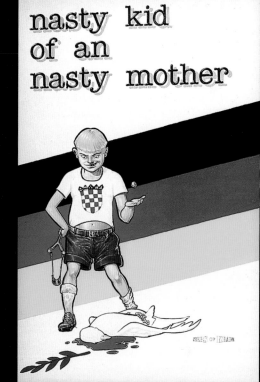

YOU CAN
PREVENT

THIS

WHY

DON'T YOU
COME IN PEACE?

SERBIAN KRAJINA REPUBLIC
MINISTRY FOR INFORMATION

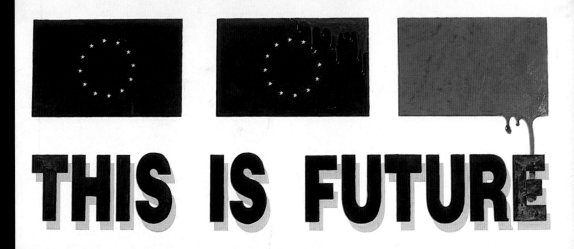

OPPOSITE LEFT:

PER SERBIAN GRAVES—AD ASTRA
Draško Mikanović et al.
Banja Luka, 1993

OPPOSITE RIGHT:

YOU HAVE VICTIMS FOR ENEMIES
Draško Mikanović et al.
Banja Luka, 1993

These posters address the international community. They express the view, still prevalent among Serbs, that Serbs are victims of an international conspiracy. Mikanović created these posters at the same time he designed the ones on the previous pages, but they were never printed.

OPPOSITE:
WHO'S NEXT?
Art Publishing
Sarajevo, 1994
Masaccio's image of Adam and Eve's expulsion from paradise, redesigned by Bojan Bahić and Sanda Hnatjuk Bahić.

FOLLOWING PAGES:
DANI *Magazine Cover*
Sarajevo, May 1994
This cover from the popular Sarajevo news magazine *DANI* associates Bosnian towns with major European and American cities. It makes the point that the fate of the "Twilight Zones" on the right very much depends on decisions made in the cities on the left.

"Adam & Eva" by Masaccio, redesign Art Publishing

INDEPENDENT MAGAZINE

DAS

BH INFORMATION MAGAZINE

NEW YORK

LONDON

MOSCOW

BRUSSELS

GENEVE

BELGRADE

TWILIGHT

ZONES

SARAJEVO 1.05.1994, No20, YEAR III, PRICE 2DM

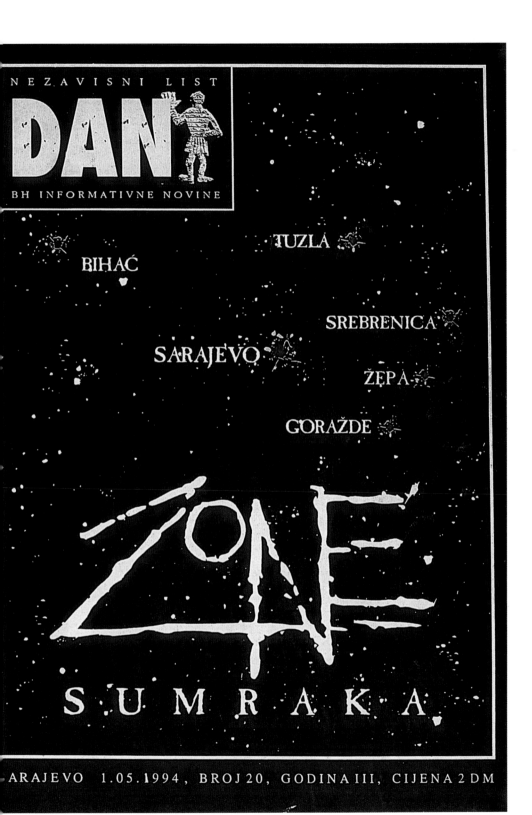

UH!
Asim Delilović
Travnik, 1993

Tensions between Bosnian Croats and Muslims in central Bosnia and Herzegovina evolved into full-scale war in April 1993. This poster expresses the shock and horror that Muslims living there felt when their former allies turned against them, deepening the conflict still further. Bosnia was now blockaded on all sides. Delilović has shaped the red-and-white Croatian *šahovnica* into the letter "U," a reference to Ustaša, the Croatian fascists of the Nazi period.

LOVE ME!
Asim Delilović
Travnik, 1993

When war broke out between Croats and Muslims, Asim Delilović was expelled from Vitez, a small town in central Bosnia. He and thousands of Muslims fled toward Travnik, the main town in the region. This poster plays on the word "love," which in Bosnian means "hunting." Delilović says that on the road to Travnik he was stopped and beaten by soldiers from the HVO. While this was happening, he remembers wondering, "Why don't these people love me?" and "Why are they hunting me?"

HOS—READY FOR HOME (HOMELAND)
Anonymous
Mostar, 1993

HSP, which stands for *Hrvatska Stranka Prava* ("Croatian Party of Right"), is an ultranationalist Croat party based in Zagreb. HSP was established in 1991 by Dobroslav Paraga, and modeled on a party of the same name that existed in the late nineteenth century. HSP is essentially a fascist organization—inspired by the Ustaša regime of Ante Pavelić—whose members believe that all Croats should be united in one state. In the early nineties HSP had a large paramilitary wing called HOS, which stands for "Croatian Defense Forces." A less literal, more accurate translation of this title is "Ready to Defend the Homeland," an Ustaša slogan from WWII. Although it sounds innocent enough, the slogan had been a battle cry during one of the most violent and brutal periods in Croatian history. Its reappearance caused widespread fear among Croatian Serbs, who remembered all too well the Serb pogroms of the 1940s.

HOS
Anonymous
Mostar, 1993

"HOS will liberate you but you alone must decide what kind of country you wish to live in."

This poster appeared prior to the Muslim-Croat split in Herzegovina, and reveals the deteriorating situation created by Croatian claims to their own ministate within the country. Note the Bosnian fleurs-de-lis at the top of the poster. After the split, this emblem was no longer used by Croats.

KUPRES—ALWAYS CROATIAN
Anonymous
Croatia, 1993

Kupres is a town in central Bosnia-Herzegovina with a large Croat population. It was much fought over in 1992 and stood as a symbol of Croatian defense.

In the winter of 1992, Tudjman placed the ultranationalist Mate Boban in power. Boban set up the Bosnian Croat parastate Herceg-Bosna, which, in line with Tudjman's own ambitions for Herzegovina, openly rejected any union with Bosnia, and attempted to secede to Croatia from Bosnia, leading to a bloody war.

ZA DOM SPREMNI

HOS

HOS ĆE VAS OSLOBODITI
A SAMI ODLUČITE
U KAKVOJ DRŽAVI ĆETE ŽIVJETI

HRVATSKO VI
OI

SPONZORI PLAKATA: Zavičajni klub »KUPRES« Za

UVIJEK HRVATSKI KUPRES

HRVATI, KUPREŠAĆI,
SVI PRIJATELJI KUPRESA,
UČINIMO SVE,
VRATIMO MIR I BLAGOSTANJE
NA NAŠ KUPRES,
S BOZJOM POMOĆI,
JEDNOM ZA SVAGDA!

Gabrijel Jurkić: VISORAVAN U CVATU
motiv kupreškog polja naslikan 1914 godine

KUPREŠKA BOJNA

E OBRANE
A KUPRES

**BRIGADA
KRALJA TOMISLAVA**

"VATSKA TISKARA« Zagreb, »VEČERNJI LIST« Zagreb, REPROSTUDIO d.o.o. ing. DRAGO REPAR, Petrova 88, Zagreb

HVO—LOVE FOR THE HOMELAND
Art Forces
Mostar, 1993
Ljubav za Dom ("Love for the Homeland") was another
Ustaša slogan popular during WWII.

OPPOSITE:
3RD (HVO) CIM REGIMENT
Anonymous
Mostar, 1993
Cim is a neighborhood on the outskirts of Mostar. Out of a
sense of patriotism, many Bosnian Croats from Herzegovina
fought against the Serbs in Croatia proper in 1991. They
returned home as seasoned fighters and prepared to
defend their homes against Serb attacks in Bosnia. They
were altogether better organized and equipped than the
Muslims.

   From April 1992 onward President Izetbegović was
concerned with the Serb onslaught in eastern Bosnia and
with defending Sarajevo. The HVO, meanwhile, was
expected to counter the Serb offensive in Herzegovina.
Initially, many Muslims enlisted in the HVO and fought
alongside Croats. This relationship deteriorated, however, as
Croat claims to an ethnically pure Croatian ministate in
Herzegovina grew.

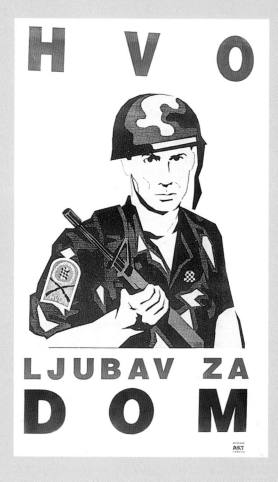

CIMSKA
III
BOJNA
2. BRIGADA

**WE ARE THE FRIENDS FROM MOSTAR—FREEDOM IS
CREATED BY ALL TOGETHER**
Nedžad Pašalić Paša
Mostar, 1993
The first part of this slogan was taken from a football cheer
for the local team, Velež, and is well known to the people of
Mostar.

OPPOSITE LEFT:
ALL FOR HERCEG-BOSNA—FOR FREEDOM
Anonymous
Croatia, 1992

OPPOSITE RIGHT:
HVO RECRUITMENT
Anonymous
Mostar, 1993
The quote on the poster reads: "Every Croat, no matter in
what part of the world he is, no matter what his personal
political views are, past faults and misconceptions were,
today wants to establish a sovereign, free state of Croatia."

Ironically, the soldier in the upper half of the poster
stands before the Stari Most, the bridge linking east and
west Mostar that was destroyed by the Croats in November
1993, in a senseless act of vandalism. Mostar is now a
divided city: West Mostar is Croat, East Mostar is Muslim.

The lower half of the poster depicts Medjugorje, a
Catholic place of pilgrimage in Herzegovina where sightings
of the Virgin Mary are frequently reported. Medjugorje and
the surrounding towns are the heartland of hard-line
Croatian nationalism. In the tourist shops of Medjugorje,
religious souvenirs are sold alongside images of Ante
Pavelić, the fascist leader of the WWII-era Croatian state.

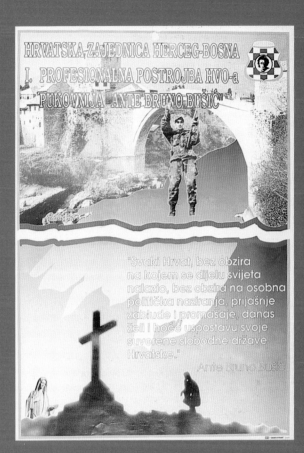

HOMAGE TO MOSTAR
Salim Obralić
Sarajevo, 1994
This poster was designed for an exhibition devoted to
Mostar's Stari Most Bridge by 25 artists. The exhibition was
an homage to the much-loved bridge after its destruction.

FOLLOWING PAGES, FROM LEFT:
BiH—IN THE HEART OF THE WORLD
Hamza Filipović
Mostar, 1993
The author of this poster died during the Muslim-Croat War.

**200,000 SOLDIERS OF THE BOSNIAN ARMY GUARANTEE
THE STATE**
Čedomir Hadžić
Mostar, 1994
This poster was printed in an edition of only 25 copies.

IZLOZBA ULUBIHa
HOMAGE MOSTARU
JANUAR 1994

B❧H

U SRCU SVIJETA
U SRCU SVIJETA
U SRCU SVIJETA U S
RCU SVIJETA U SRCU
SVIJETA U SRCU SVIJET
A U SRCU SVIJETA U SRCU
SVIJETA U SRCU SVIJETA U
SRCU SVIJETA U SRCU SVIJETA
U SRCU SVIJETA U SRCU SVIJETA U SR
CU SVIJETA U SRCU SVIJETA U SRCU SVIJ

200000 boraca
armije
bosne i hercegovine
garant
državnosti

OPPOSITE:
TOP LEFT:
AGAINST EVIL—FOR A FREE BiH
Ismet Hrvanović
Tuzla, 1992

TOP RIGHT:
LET'S OVERRUN THEM!
Anonymous
Zenica, 1994

BOTTOM LEFT:
LET'S DIG TO VICTORY
ABiH Press Center
Sarajevo, 1992
This poster was produced to encourage young Bosnian army fighters to defend themselves by digging trenches.

BOTTOM RIGHT:
BOSNIAN ARMY ON BOSNIA'S BORDERS
ABiH Press Center
Sarajevo, 1993
We came across this poster in the house of collector Zlatko Serdarević on the (Muslim) east side of Mostar. Serdarević rummaged around for quite a while before digging out this work from his massive stock.

Above, there was a large, hastily fixed hole in the ceiling. A mortar had hit the house in 1994, passing through the roof and embedding itself in the floor. Its tail and fins were still sticking out of the carpet.

PROTIV ZLA ZA SLOBODNU BOSNU I HERCEGOVINU

ARMIJA
REPUBLIKE
BOSNE I HERCEGOVINE

PREGAZIMO IH!

KOPAJMO DO POBJEDE

BOSANSKA VOJSKA
NA BOSANSKIM GRANICAMA

15 APRIL—REPUBLIC OF BiH ARMY DAY
Salim Obralić
Sarajevo, 1994

FREEDOM
Zdravko Novak
Tuzla, 1992

CRIMINALS—THEY WILL NOT FORGIVE YOU
TO

Sarajevo, 1992
This poster was produced by the Territorial Defense as a warning that organized criminals operating within Sarajevo would not be tolerated. The girl is the daughter of the photographer Kemal Hadžić.

DEDICATED TO VASE MISKIN STREET—STREET OF SPITE
TO

Sarajevo, 1992
On May 27, 1992, seventeen people were killed in a narrow Sarajevan street while they were lining up for bread. Television pictures of the atrocity were broadcast around the world. It was perhaps the first event that brought the brutal reality of the Bosnian War into Western living rooms.

The Serbian leadership denied that Serb forces fired the mortars. In Belgrade, the press blamed Muslim paramilitary units, claiming that they had shelled their own people in order to encourage anti-Serb feelings, and had then swapped the bodies of Serbs killed there for Muslim and Croat corpses, a cynical fabrication.

NO ONE'S (CANDLE) EVER BURNT UNTIL DAWN
TO

Sarajevo, 1992
This slogan is derived from a popular saying that nothing lasts forever. The two candles are labeled JNA and CCCC, meaning "Only Unity Saves the Serbs."

This poster is based on a Polish poster designed in the late seventies by Jacek Ćwikđa.

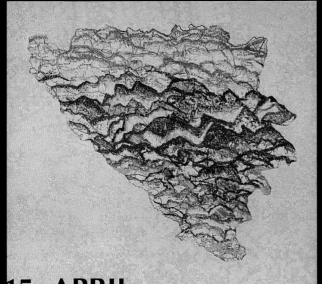

15. APRIL
DAN ARMIJE
REPUBLIKE
BOSNE I HERCEGOVINE

SLOBODA

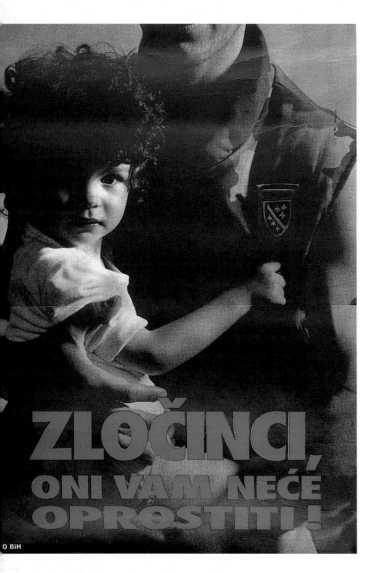

Ničija nije do zore gorjela!

TO Bi

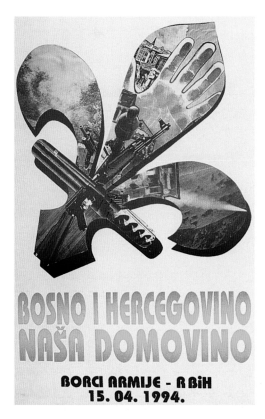

ABOVE LEFT:
ANNIVERSARY OF THE VICTORY AT VIS
Nijaz Omerović
Gračanica, 1993

ABOVE RIGHT:
BiH—OUR HOMELAND
Irfan Handukić
Zenica, 1994

BOTTOM:
LET'S ALL JOIN IN TO DEFEND BiH
Irfan Handukić
Zenica, 1994
The caption at the bottom reads: "This is how those who didn't succeed in defending themselves ended up."

OPPOSITE TOP:
HAPPILY TOWARDS FREEDOM (ABiH)
Fuad Kasumović
Tuzla, 1995

OPPOSITE BOTTOM:
DEFEND BOSNIA AND HERZEGOVINA
Irfan Handukić
Zenica, 1994
This ABiH poster calls for assistance from foreign air powers.

ARMIJA
REPUBLIKE BOSNE I HERCEGOVINE
15. april '92. 15. april '95

Sretno do slobode

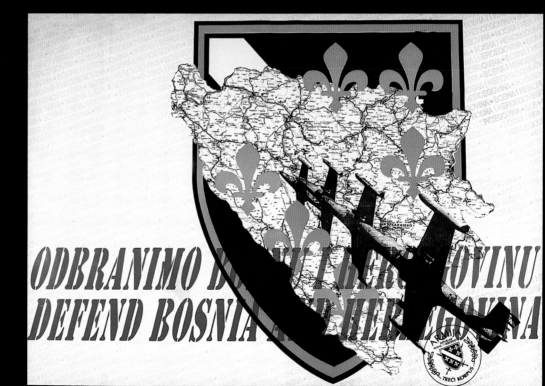

ODBRANIMO BOSNU I HERCEGOVINU
DEFEND BOSNIA AND HERCEGOVINA

DAN ARMIJE REPUBLIKE BOSNE I HERCEGOVINE

15. APRIL

CRNI LABUDOVI 4.4.'94.

DISUNITED NATIONS OF
BOSNIA AND HERZEGOVINA

ABOVE:
DISUNITED NATIONS OF BiH
TRIO
Sarajevo, 1993
This redesign of the UN logo was created after the Vance-Owen Plan of 1993 was put forward, seriously worsening the war. The plan proposed ethnic cantons that would be governed by the majority populations in each. Although the plan was not implemented, it encouraged ethnic purging by Serbs and Croats, who attempted to homogenize what they saw as their territories.

PREVIOUS LEFT:
ARMY DAY
ABiH Press Center
Sarajevo, 1996

PREVIOUS RIGHT:
BLACK SWANS
Anonymous
Tuzla, 1994
The Black Swans were an infamous paramilitary unit. They operated primarily in central Bosnia, where they were exclusively Croat, and were accused of appalling acts of brutality and terror. In the Tuzla region, however, the Black Swans were a joint Muslim-Croat paramilitary that fought, covertly, alongside government forces of the ABiH.

OPPOSITE:
THIS IS MY HOMELAND!
ABiH Press Center
Sarajevo, 1993
During the Bosnian War, foreign powers put forward various peace plans, all of which proposed partitioning the country along ethnic lines. Democratic Bosnians were adamant that Bosnia should not be divided.

The map in the top right-hand corner of this poster depicts the peace plan proposed by David Owen and Thorvald Stoltenberg in September 1993. The map in the opposite corner appears to be the Contact Group plan of July 1994. The slogan over both maps reads, "This Is Not My Homeland."

FOLLOWING PAGES:
DANI *Magazine Cover*
Sarajevo, January 1994
The question posed on both sides of this cover refers to the Dayton Accord that ended the war between Muslims and Croats in Bosnia, and that led to the formation of the Muslim-Croat Federation. The left side shows the Yugoslav flag, now used only by the Federal Republic of Yugoslavia, stamped with a swastika.

OVO NIJE MOJA DOMOVINA...

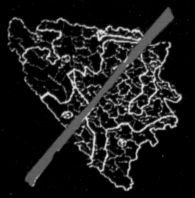

NI OVO NIJE MOJA DOMOVINA...

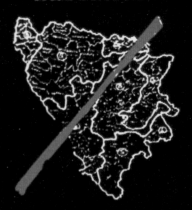

OVO JE
MOJA DOMOVINA!

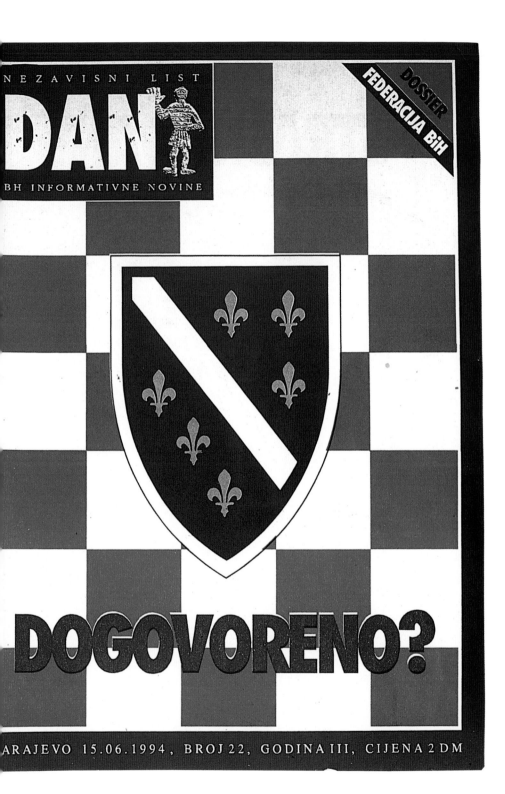

NEZAVISNI LIST

DAN

BH INFORMATIVNE NOVINE

DOSSIER
FEDERACIJA BiH

DOGOVORENO?

ARAJEVO 15.06.1994, BROJ 22, GODINA III, CIJENA 2 DM

UNTOUCHABLE
Art Publishing
Sarajevo, 1994

OPPOSITE:
PIPE OF PEACE
Art Publishing
Sarajevo, 1994
This poster makes a play on René Magritte's famous
painting *Ceci n'est pas une pipe* ("This is not a pipe").

FOLLOWING PAGES:
DANI *Magazine Cover*
Sarajevo, December 1994
This cover, designed by TRIO, features a calendar that
counts the days of the Sarajevo siege.

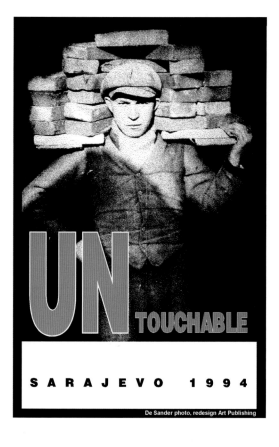

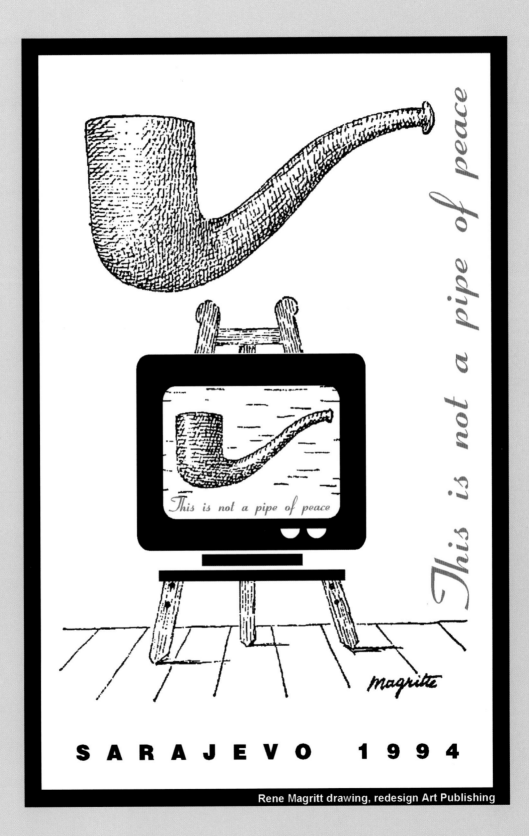

This is not a pipe of peace

This is not a pipe of peace

SARAJEVO 1994

Rene Magritt drawing, redesign Art Publishing

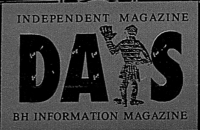

INTERVIEW: ALIJA IZETBEGOVIĆ

INDEPENDENT MAGAZINE

DAYS

BH INFORMATION MAGAZINE

Sarajevo 1994

Januar
Po	Ut	Sr	Če	Pe	Su	Ne
					637	638
639	640	641	642	643	644	645
646	647	648	649	650	651	652
653	654	655	656	657	658	659
660	661	662	663	664	665	666
667						

Februar
Po	Ut	Sr	Če	Pe	Su	Ne
	668	669	670	671	672	673
674	675	676	677	678	679	680
681	682	683	684	685	686	687
688	689	690	691	692	693	694
695						

Mart
Po	Ut	Sr	Če	Pe	Su	Ne
	696	697	698	699	700	701
702	703	704	705	706	707	708
709	710	711	712	713	714	715
716	717	718	719	720	721	722
723	724	725	726			

April
Po	Ut	Sr	Če	Pe	Su	Ne
					727	728	729
730	731	732	733	734	735	736
737	738	739	740	741	742	743
744	745	746	747	748	749	750
751	752	753	754	755	756	

Maj
Po	Ut	Sr	Če	Pe	Su	Ne
						757
758	759	760	761	762	763	764
765	766	767	768	769	770	771
772	773	774	775	776	777	778
779	780	781	782	783	784	785
786	787					

Juni
Po	Ut	Sr	Če	Pe	Su	Ne
		788	789	790	791	792
793	794	795	796	797	798	799
800	801	802	803	804	805	806
807	808	809	810	811	812	813
814	815	816	817			

Juli
Po	Ut	Sr	Če	Pe	Su	Ne
				818	819	820
821	822	823	824	825	826	827
828	829	830	831	832	833	834
835	836	837	838	839	840	841
842	843	844	845	846	847	848

August
Po	Ut	Sr	Če	Pe	Su	Ne
849	850	851	852	853	854	855
856	857	858	859	860	861	862
863	864	865	866	867	868	869
870	871	872	873	874	875	876
877	878	879				

Septembar
Po	Ut	Sr	Če	Pe	Su	Ne
				880	881	882	883
884	885	886	887	888	889	890
891	892	893	894	895	896	897
898	899	900	901	902	903	904
905	906	907	908	909		

Oktobar
Po	Ut	Sr	Če	Pe	Su	Ne
					910	911
912	913	914	915	916	917	918
919	920	921	922	923	924	925
926	927	928	929	930	931	932
933	934	935	936	937	938	939
940						

Novembar
Po	Ut	Sr	Če	Pe	Su	Ne
	941	942	943	944	945	946
947	948	949	950	951	952	953
954	955	956	957	958	959	960
961	962	963	964	965	966	967
968	969	970				

Decembar
Po	Ut	Sr	Če	Pe	Su	Ne
			971	972	973	974
975	976	977	978	979	980	981
982	983	984	985	986	987	988
989	990	991	992	993	994	995
996	997	998	999	1000	1001	

Go Ahead

4. April 1992 – 1. January 1995

SARAJEVO, 31.12.1994. No 27, YEAR III, PRICE 2 DM

NEZAVISNI MAGAZIN

DAN

BH INFORMATIVNI MAGAZIN

INTERVJU: ALIJA IZETBEGOVIĆ

Sarajevo 1995

Januar

Ne	Po	Ut	Sr	Če	Pe	Su
1002	1003	1004	1005	1006	1007	1008
1009	1010	1011	1012	1013	1014	1015
1016	1017	1018	1019	1020	1021	1022
1023	1024	1025	1026	1027	1028	1029
1030	1031	1032				

Februar

Ne	Po	Ut	Sr	Če	Pe	Su
			1033	1034	1035	1036
1037	1038	1039	1040	1041	1042	1043
1044	1045	1046	1047	1048	1049	1050
1051	1052	1053	1054	1055	1056	1057
1058	1059	1060				

Mart

Ne	Po	Ut	Sr	Če	Pe	Su
			1061	1062	1063	1064
1065	1066	1067	1068	1069	1070	1071
1072	1073	1074	1075	1076	1077	1078
1079	1080	1081	1082	1083	1084	1085
1086	1087	1088	1089	1090	1091	

April

Ne	Po	Ut	Sr	Če	Pe	Su
						1092
1093	1094	1095	1096	1097	1098	1099
1100	1101	1102	1103	1104	1105	1106
1107	1108	1109	1110	1111	1112	1113
1114	1115	1116	1117	1118	1119	1120
1121						

Maj

Ne	Po	Ut	Sr	Če	Pe	Su
	1122	1123	1124	1125	1126	1127
1128	1129	1130	1131	1132	1133	1134
1135	1136	1137	1138	1139	1140	1141
1142	1143	1144	1145	1146	1147	1148
1149	1150	1151	1152			

Juni

Ne	Po	Ut	Sr	Če	Pe	Su
				1153	1154	1155
1156	1157	1158	1159	1160	1161	1162
1163	1164	1165	1166	1167	1168	1169
1170	1171	1172	1173	1174	1175	1176
1177	1178	1179	1180	1181	1182	

Juli

Ne	Po	Ut	Sr	Če	Pe	Su
						1183
1184	1185	1186	1187	1188	1189	1190
1191	1192	1193	1194	1195	1196	1197
1198	1199	1200	1201	1202	1203	1204
1205	1206	1207	1208	1209	1210	1211
1212	1213					

August

Ne	Po	Ut	Sr	Če	Pe	Su
		1214	1215	1216	1217	1218
1219	1220	1221	1222	1223	1224	1225
1226	1227	1228	1229	1230	1231	1232
1233	1234	1235	1236	1237	1238	1239
1240	1241	1242	1243	1244		

Septembar

Ne	Po	Ut	Sr	Če	Pe	Su
					1245	1246
1247	1248	1249	1250	1251	1252	1253
1254	1255	1256	1257	1258	1259	1260
1261	1262	1263	1264	1265	1266	1267
1268	1269	1270	1271	1272	1273	1274

Oktobar

Ne	Po	Ut	Sr	Če	Pe	Su
1275	1276	1277	1278	1279	1280	1281
1282	1283	1284	1285	1286	1287	1288
1289	1290	1291	1292	1293	1294	1295
1296	1297	1298	1299	1300	1301	1302
1303	1304	1305				

Novembar

Ne	Po	Ut	Sr	Če	Pe	Su
			1306	1307	1308	1309
1310	1311	1312	1313	1314	1315	1316
1317	1318	1319	1320	1321	1322	1323
1324	1325	1326	1327	1328	1329	1330
1331	1332	1333	1334	1335		

Decembar

Ne	Po	Ut	Sr	Če	Pe	Su
					1336	1337
1338	1339	1340	1341	1342	1343	1344
1345	1346	1347	1348	1349	1350	1351
1352	1353	1354	1355	1356	1357	1358
1359	1360	1361	1362	1363	1364	1365
1366						

Idemo dalje

4. April 1992 – 1. Januar 1996

SARAJEVO, 31.12.1994. BROJ 27, GODINA III, CIJENA 2 DM

WHO FUCKED THE CULTURE UP?
TRIO
Sarajevo, 1995

This poster was produced for the Sarajevo Winter Festival, which is held at the beginning of each year. This arts festival began in 1984, the year the Winter Olympics took place in Sarajevo, and was held each year of the siege, against overwhelming odds.

Sarajevo is home to most of Bosnia's artists and designers. Although many left during the war, many more stayed and contributed to the rich and varied artistic life of the city. Inevitably, images of war and death occupied a central place in the art produced during the siege. Much of the work protests against the injustice of the war and calls for international attention.

Many foreign artists, theater directors, actors, musicians, and designers responded to this call, visiting Sarajevo and lending their talents and voices to those who lived there. Although this meant that Sarajevo had a fertile artistic life, the international publicity the city received condemned many other Bosnian towns to relative obscurity.

Who Fucked the Culture up?

SARAJEVO '95

DESIGN TRIO SARAJEVO

UNTITLED
Fuad Hadžihalilović
Sarajevo, 1995

OPPOSITE:
SARAJEVO ALPHABET
TRIO
Sarajevo, 1994

UNTITLED
TRIO
Sarajevo, 1993

OPPOSITE:
STOP
Enis Selimović
Sarajevo, 1994

FOLLOWING PAGES, FROM LEFT:
TOP LEFT:
EVERYTHING IS POSSIBLE!!!
Art Publishing
Sarajevo, 1995

TOP RIGHT:
SARAJEVO—CULTURAL CAPITAL OF EUROPE
Dino Malović
Sarajevo, 1994

BOTTOM LEFT:
UNTITLED
Fikret Libovać
Sarajevo, 1995

BOTTOM RIGHT:
SARAJEVO WINTER
Salim Obralić
Sarajevo, 1993

RIGHT PAGE:
UNTITLED
Dino Malović
Sarajevo, 1994

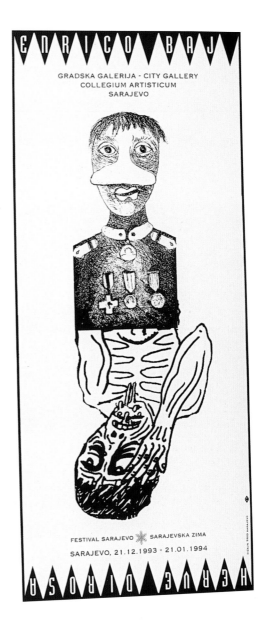

FESTIVAL SARAJEVO

sarajevska zima '94   sarajevo winter '94

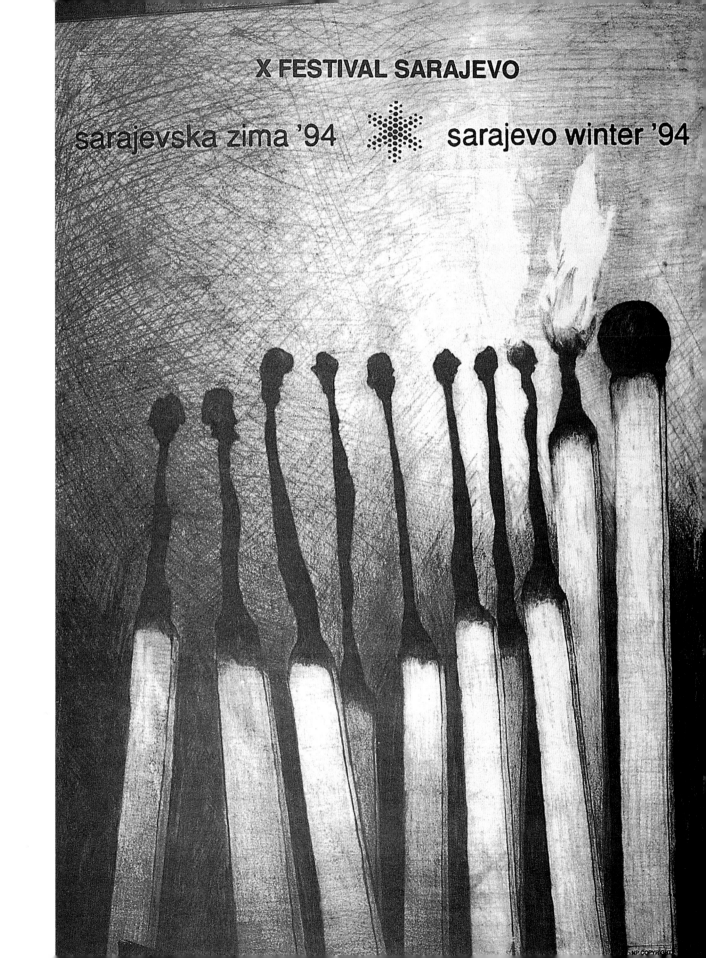

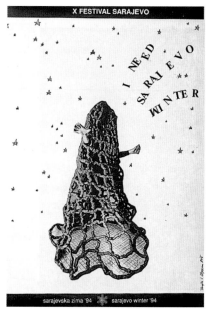

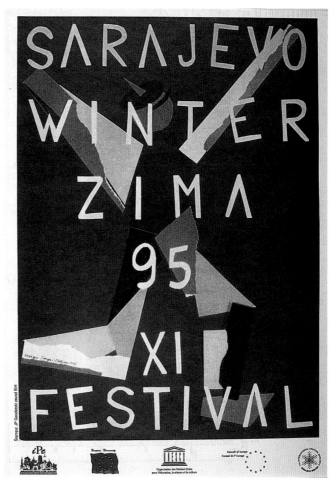

PREVIOUS PAGES:
LEFT PAGE:
TOP LEFT:
UNTITLED
Avdo Žiga
Sarajevo, 1995

TOP RIGHT:
I NEED SARAJEVO WINTER
Stjepan Roš
Sarajevo, 1994

BOTTOM LEFT:
UNTITLED
Andreas Pfeiffer
Sarajevo, 1995

BOTTOM RIGHT:
UNTITLED
Mehmed Zaimović
Sarajevo, 1996

RIGHT PAGE:
LEFT:
OPERETA EUROPA
Nusret Pašić
Sarajevo, 1995

RIGHT:
SARAJEVO WINTER
Tanja and Stjepan Roš
Sarajevo, 1995

OPPOSITE TOP:
AJ
Enis Selimović
Sarajevo, 1992
Aj is an expression of physical pain or shock, akin to "ouch" in English.

OPPOSITE BOTTOM:
ARTISTS OF SARAJEVO FOR A FREE BiH
Dževad Hozo
Sarajevo, 1992
The artists listed on this poster held a joint exhibition of work in Sarajevo at a gallery belonging to the Army of Bosnia-Herzegovina. This was a symbolic way for the artists to state that they supported the army and the elected government in Sarajevo in its fight against Serb aggression. Heavy shelling prevented many of them from attending the photo session for the poster outside the Sarajevo Academy of Fine Art.

SAR**A**JEVO

1992 '93

UMJETNICI SARAJEVA ZA SLOBODNU BOSNU I HERCEGOVINU

Mustafa Skopljak	Salem Obralić	Čulić Dragan	Sućeska Hasan
Seid Hasanefendić	Pašić Nusret	Avdo Žiga	Mirsada Baljić	Sead Čizmić	Dževad Hozo	Edin Numankadić
	Esad Muftić		

Arifović Nedim
Acković-Čišić Nina
Bostandžić Smail
Češljar Suad
Gavrić Alma
Gavrić Stjepo
Hozo Irfan
Karamatić Renata
Karišik Husein
Kasapović Mile
Libovac Fikret

Alma Suljević
Ljubović Ibrahim
Malović Edin
Muhić Hamzalija
Mujezinović Saida
Kalcina Ivan
Kovač Ana
Ramić Afan
Tadić Radoslav
Vrana Elma
Zaimović Mehmed
Walldeg Petar

Superman logo redesigned by "Trio" -Sarajevo

SARAJEVO
WORLD GREATEST
ADVENTURE STRIP
CHARACTER!

Lichtenstein's "Hopeless" - Redesign by "Trio" - Sarajevo

ABOVE LEFT:
SUPERMAN
TRIO
Sarajevo, 1994
The *DC Comics* character, redesigned.

ABOVE RIGHT:
HOPELESS
TRIO
Sarajevo, 1994
Inspired by Roy Lichtenstein.

OPPOSITE:
CAMPBELL'S SOUP
TRIO
Sarajevo, 1994
A reinterpretation of the pop art painting
by Andy Warhol.

FOLLOWING PAGES, FROM LEFT:
SCREAM
TRIO
Sarajevo, 1993
A redesign of the famous painting by Edvard Munch.

MONA LISA
TRIO
Sarajevo, 1993
After Leonardo da Vinci.

X FESTIVAL SARAJEVO

"Scream" redesign by "Trio" - Sarajevo

 sarajevska zima '94 sarajevo winter '94

"Mona Lisa" redesign by "Trio" - Sarajevo

SARAJEVO 1993

IT WAS HONORABLE TO LIVE WITH SARAJEVO
DANI *Magazine*
Sarajevo, 1993
The slogan "It Was Honourable to Live with Tito" was popular after Tito's death in 1980. Here Tito's coffin is replaced with Sarajevo's damaged buildings. Around them stands a cluster of JNA officers. The audience is a photomontage of faces relevant to the times, among them Milošević, Šešelj, Karadžić, Tudjman, and Izetbegović. This poster was distributed as a free insert in *DANI*.

INDEPENDANT MAGAZINE
DAYS
BH INFORMATION MAGAZINE

BILO JE ČASNO
ŽIVJETI SA SARAJEVOM...

NEZAVISNI LIST
DAN
BH INFORMATIVNE NOVINE

BACK TO THE FUTURE
Art Publishing
Sarajevo, 1994

BACK TO THE FUTURE

IN BOSNIA

design Art Publishing

1ST ANNIVERSARY—MAY 25, 1995
Printcom
Tuzla, 1996

At 9:00 P.M. on May 25, 1995—National Youth Day—Serb forces in the hills above Tuzla fired a shell that landed in the center of an old square called Kapija, where young people regularly gathered to chat and drink coffee. The shell exploded in their midst. Seventy-one people died, most of them between the ages of eighteen and twenty-five. More than one hundred were injured.

So appalling were the pictures that broadcasters around the world refused to screen the material. Partly for this reason, the massacre received little international attention. Nearly all those killed were buried together in a special cemetery, and the site where the shell fell is now marked with a plaque.

FOLLOWING PAGES:
DANI *Magazine Cover*
Sarajevo, August 1995

Besieged throughout the war, the eastern Bosnian towns of Srebrenica and Žepa were declared safe areas by the United Nations in April 1993.

They turned out to be two of the most unsafe places in Bosnia. On July 11, 1995, Serb forces around Srebrenica, led by General Ratko Mladić, overran the town. The Serbs met no resistance from the Dutch UNPROFOR troops stationed there. Twenty-three thousand Muslim women and children were expelled.

INTERVIEW: BAKIR ALISPAHIĆ

INDEPENDENT MAGAZINE

DAN

BH INFORMATION MAGAZINE

EXPELLED

SARAJEVO AUGUST 1995, No 34, YEAR IV, PRICE 2 DM

NEZAVISNI MAGAZIN

DAN

BH INFORMATIVNI MAGAZIN

INTERVJU:
BAKIR ALISPAHIĆ

PROGNANI

ARAJEVO AVGUST/KOLOVOZ 1995, BROJ 34, GODINA IV, CIJENA 2 DM

KAPIJA
Edin Derviševič
Tuzla, 1995

FOLLOWING PAGES:
DANI *Magazine Cover*
Sarajevo, August 1995
In the days following the abandonment of Srebrenica,
the first news started to appear about the fate of the town's
male population. Some had been hunted down in the
forests as they tried to escape. Many more were separated
from their families and taken away. All those caught were
executed within days. The number of dead is now believed
to be around 8,000. This crime was the worst single atrocity
committed in Europe since the end of WWII.

On July 25, two weeks after Srebrenica was captured,
the neighboring town of Žepa suffered a similar fate.

Tuzlanskoj mladosti od Edina Derviševića | PrintCom-a

INDEPENDENT MAGAZINE

DAN

BH INFORMATION MAGAZINE

ONCE AGAIN!

SARAJEVO   SEPTEMBER 1995 , No 35, YEAR IV, PRICE 2 DM

NEZAVISNI MAGAZIN

DAN

BH INFORMATIVNI MAGAZIN

PONOVO!

RAJEVO SEPTEMBAR/RUJAN 1995, BROJ 35, GODINA IV, CIJENA 2 DM

VRATIMO IM VJERU U ŽIVOT

LET'S GIVE THEM BACK THEIR FAITH IN LIFE
Adin Šadić
Tuzla, 1995
The vast majority of refugees from Srebrenica ended up living in the Tuzla region. This poster was commissioned by Bosnian President Izetbegović's ruling party.

OPPOSITE:
BIRDS
Jasminko Arnautović
Tuzla, 1995
The posters of Tuzla-based designer Jasminko Arnautović always address issues of nationalism and tolerance. During the war Tuzla largely retained its multiethnic mix, thanks to a progressive mayor and the common decency of its citizens.

Arnautović was questioned by police about this poster, as it appeared shortly after the events in Srebrenica and Žepa. Authorities mistakenly believed that the birds represented refugees attacking Tuzla, and that it was meant as a sarcastic retort to the poster by Adin Šadić on the previous page. Actually, Arnautović intended it as a warning against the constant danger posed by nationalism of all kinds. The poster was commissioned by the Tuzla Citizens' Forum, as were many of Arnautović's posters. The statue is of a salt miner, one of the symbols of the town.

FOLLOWING PAGES:
DANI *Magazine Cover*
Sarajevo, November 1994
On August 28, 1995, Serb forces around Sarajevo fired a mortar that landed near the market square, killing thirty-seven people. Three days later, after years of indecision, NATO began bombing Serb military targets around Sarajevo and throughout Serb-held territory. The campaign lasted two weeks, driving heavy Serb artillery away from Sarajevo and weakening Serb forces throughout Bosnia. The bombings set the stage for the Dayton negotiations that ended the war.

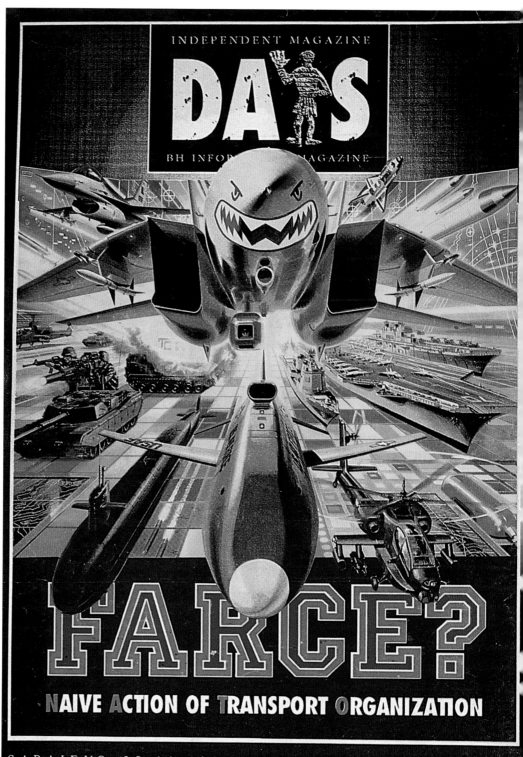

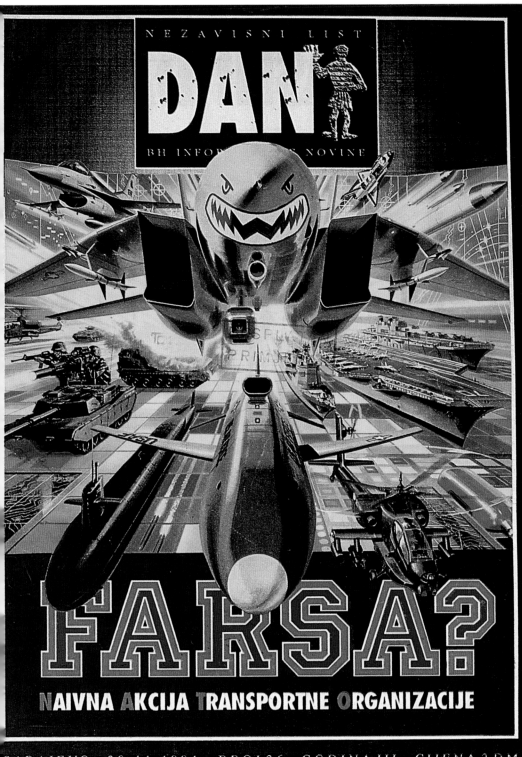

END OF WAR!?
Asim Delilović
Travnik, 1996

In Bosnian the word *rat* means "war." Delilović uses it to mimic the sound of a machine gun firing. The exclamation and question marks express the skepticism felt by many Bosnians when the Dayton peace accords were signed in November 1995.

OPPOSITE:
BOSNIA
Čedomir Kostović
USA, 1995

A wry comment on the Dayton peace agreements, Kostović's poster compares the dismemberment of Bosnia into three ethnic parts (Muslim, Serb, and Croat) to the dissection of a violin.

BOSNIA

DEYTONATION
Asim Delilović
Travnik, 1996

This poster represents a pun on the word "Dayton," spelled phonetically as it would be in Bosnian, and "detonation."

The Dayton agreement guaranteed the right of more than two million refugees to return home. But as 1996 wore on, it became obvious that this was not going to be an easy process. Nationalists and war criminals were still in power all over the country, especially in the Republika Srpska. Many of the authorities the agreement relied on for cooperation were the same people who had fought so hard to create ethnically pure states. They had no intention of wrecking their chances of retaining power by allowing refugees to return to their homes.

The towns listed in this poster became flash points as refugees attempted to return. There were riots in Stolac and Jusići, which were under the control of Croats and Serbs respectively. In Mostar, Croats continued to expel Muslims from the west of the city. Brčko was a special case: It was the only town in Bosnia whose status was left open at Dayton. Several years after the agreement, this issue was "resolved" by placing Brčko under the control of the international community.

DEjTONACIJE

Stolac, Jusići, Mostar, Brčko...

BRČKO—THE TEST OF HUMANITY
Jasminko Arnautović
Tuzla, 1998

Brčko is in the north of Bosnia, near the Croatian border.
Before the war it had a majority Muslim population, with a
sizable Croat population and a Serb minority. During the
war Serb forces removed all non-Serbs from Brčko, killing
thousands. At present it forms a corridor linking the eastern
and western areas of the Republika Srpska, and Serbs are
adamant that it should remain a part of their territory.
Brčko is also of vital strategic interest to the Muslim-Croat
Federation (since it would give them access to the Sava
River and concomitant trading benefits).

Many people see the Brčko region as the most
dangerous and controversial in Bosnia. In March 1999 the
international community proclaimed Brčko to be a special
multiethnic district. Many Serbs, as well as Muslims,
reacted angrily against this ruling. In October 2000 there
was a serious outbreak of violence in Brčko: A thousand
Serb students rampaged through the town, smashing
Muslim properties and demanding the expulsion of
Muslims from Brčko.

The three butterfly nets in this poster represent the
interests of the three main nationalities in Bosnia, and the
butterfly incorporates the colors associated with the three
factions. The poster was commissioned by the Tuzla
Citizens' Forum.

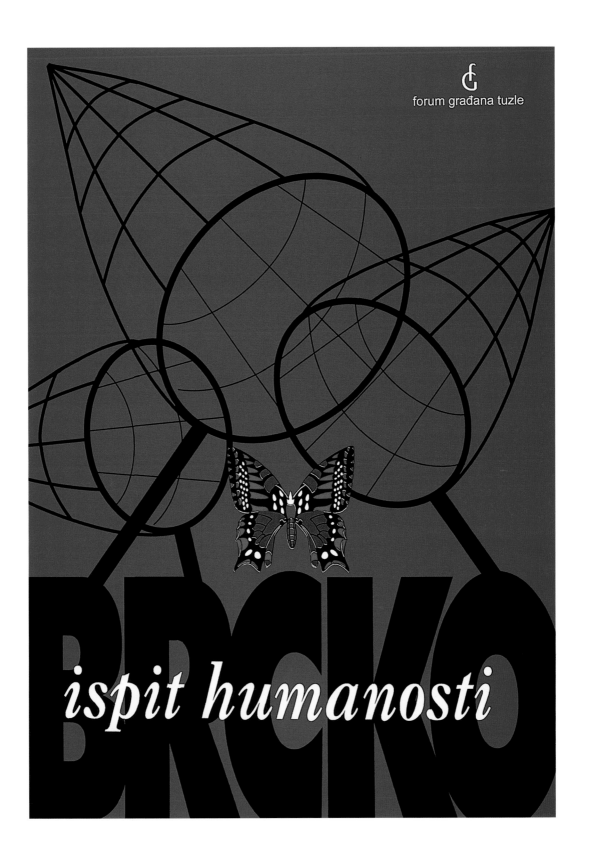

forum građana tuzle

BRCKO

ispit humanosti

**BRČKO IS SERBIAN AND IS GOING TO STAY SERBIAN—
WE KEEP OUR WORD—ARKAN**
Serbian Unity Party
Brčko, 1996

In 1996 the Serb paramilitary leader Arkan metamorphosed into a politician. After conducting terror campaigns throughout Bosnia and Croatia with his "Tigers," he actually received funding for his party from the European Community. He ran in the first elections in Bosnia, held in September 1996. He was later banned from political office in Bosnia, and the international community withdrew his funding. Later still, he took part in the war in Kosovo, before being assassinated in a hotel lobby in Belgrade.

OPPOSITE:
ARKAN ELECTION POSTERS
Photograph by Alina Boboc
Republika Srpska, 1996

REFUCHESS
Art Publishing
Sarajevo, 1994

OPPOSITE:
LET ME GO HOME
Jasminko Arnautović
Tuzla, 1998

More than two million people lost their homes during the fighting in Bosnia. This image speaks about the right of refugees and the internally displaced to return home. It was produced in early 1998, more than two years after the Dayton agreement was signed and the conflict ended. Those brave enough to return home first had to cope with a complex bureaucracy. This poster was commissioned by the Tuzla Citizens' Forum.

RADO-OUT
Novi Prelom *Magazine Cover*
Banja Luka, July 1996

Novi Prelom is an independent news magazine published in Banja Luka, which is often critical of the Republika Srpska's nationalist leadership. It shut down during the war but reopened in late 1995.

In Bosnian *van* means "out." The image is a photomontage of Radovan Karadžić's face, on the left, and Biljana Plavšić's, on the right. Plavšić was a staunch Karadžić ally throughout the war. When the war ended and Karadžić was indicted for war crimes, Plavšić seized leadership of Karadžić's SDS (Serb Democratic Party). She became president of the Republika Srpska in 1996, and was supported by the international community, which initially saw her as more cooperative than other Bosnian Serb politicians. However, much to the horror of the international community, she lost the 1998 presidential elections to the ultranationalist Serb Radical Party.

The *Novi Prelom* cover implies that despite her new image as a "democrat," Plavšić was fatally compromised by her relationship with Karadžić. Indeed, she held views so extreme that even Milošević once said she should be locked away. Plavšić was a practicing biologist before the war, and often expressed the view that Muslims were "genetically inferior" to Serbs, and that ethnic cleansing was a "natural phenomenon."

Eventually Plavšić turned herself over to the International Tribunal in The Hague, correctly assuming that her name was on a secret wanted list. She was charged with genocide, war crimes, and other offenses, and at the time of this writing is the most senior Bosnian Serb official awaiting trial.

WE DID NOT BLEED IN VAIN
Draško Mikanović
Banja Luka, 1996

This poster was a powerful criticism of the SDS, its policies, and its leadership from within the Republika Srpska.
The slogan at the bottom reads "The SDS Cashed In."

WE ARE CARRYING ON!
SDS
Pale, 1996

After the war in Bosnia ended and Radovan Karadžić was indicted for war crimes, his political power waned. In response, posters supporting Karadžić began to appear, some in Bosnian and some in English, aimed at the international community.

Since the Dayton agreement barred indicted war criminals from holding political office, none of the posters carried the logo of the SDS, which Karadžić formerly led. It is widely believed, however, that these posters were produced by the SDS.

OPPOSITE:
HE MEANS PEACE
SDS
Photograph by Daoud Sarhandi
Republika Srpska, 1997

This is one of several absurd English-language posters that appeared with Radovan Karadžić's portrait. Others in the series read "Don't Touch Him" and "He Is Freedom."

FOLLOWING PAGES, FROM LEFT:
WITH TRADITION INTO THE FUTURE
SDS
Pale, 1998

The three faces on the screen are those of Saint Sava (the patron saint of Serbs), Nikola Tesla (the Serbian-American scientist), and Vuk Karadžić (a nineteenth-century linguist and writer). The fingers of the child's right hand form the traditional, three-fingered Serb salute.

HAPPY, PEACEFUL NEW YEAR '96
Novi Prelom
Banja Luka, 1996

УСПЈЕЛИ СМО, НАСТАВЉАМО!

С ТРАДИЦИЈОМ У БУДУЋНОСТ !

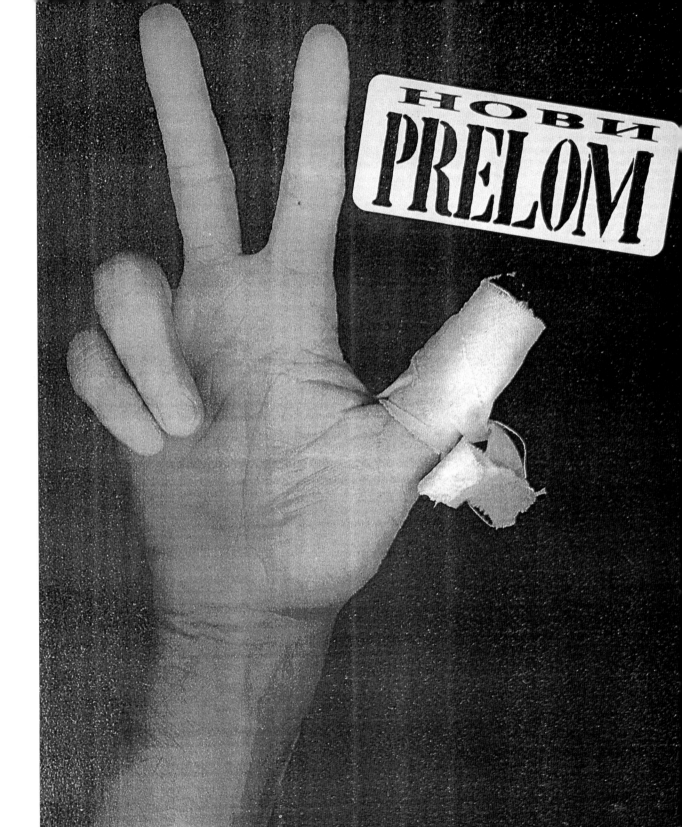

WANTED—PERSONS INDICTED FOR WAR CRIMES
ICTY
As of February 12, 1998
This poster was released by the International Criminal
Tribunal for the former Yugoslavia. Faces were filled in as
photographs were acquired by the tribunal. The poster
appeared across Bosnia-Herzegovina.

PERSONS INDICTED FOR WAR CRIMES

WARRANTS FOR THEIR ARREST ARE HELD BY THEIR RESPECTIVE CAPITALS

IF YOU ENCOUNTER ANY OF THESE INDICTED WAR CRIMINALS IN THE COURSE OF YOUR REGULAR DUTIES AND THE SITUATION PERMITS, DETAIN THEM AND CONTACT YOUR CHAIN OF COMMAND!

Updated as of: 12 Feb '98

Updated as of: 12 Feb '98

MIRKO BABIĆ · NENAD BANOVIĆ · PREDRAG BANOVIĆ · GORAN BOROVNICA · RANKO ČEŠIĆ · DAMIR DOŠEN · DRAGAN FUŠTAR · DRAGAN GAGOVIĆ · MOMČILO GRUBAN

JANKO JANJIĆ · GOJKO JANKOVIĆ · RADOVAN KARADŽIĆ · DUŠAN KNEŽEVIĆ · DRAGAN KONDIĆ · MILOJICA KOS · PREDRAG KOSTIĆ · RADOMIR KOVAČ · DRAGOLJUB KUNARAC

DRAGAN KULUNDŽIJA · MIROSLAV KVOČKA · GORAN LAJIĆ · ZORAN MARINIĆ · MILAN MARTIĆ · ŽELJKO MEAKIĆ · SLOBODAN MILJKOVIĆ · RATKO MLADIĆ · MILE MRKŠIĆ

DRAGAN NIKOLIĆ · NEDELJKO PASPALJ · MILAN PAVLIĆ · DRAGOLJUB PRCAĆ · MILUTIN POPOVIĆ · BRAĐENKO PREDOJEVIĆ · MLADEN RADIĆ · MIROSLAV RADIĆ · IVICA RAJIĆ

DRAGOMIR ŠAPONJA · ŽELJKO SAVIĆ · DUŠKO SIKIRICA · BLAGOJE SIMIĆ · MILAN SIMIĆ · VESELIN ŠLJIVANČANIN · RADOVAN STANKOVIĆ · MIROSLAV TADIĆ · NEDELJKO TIMARAC

STEVAN TODOROVIĆ · ZORAN VUKOVIĆ · SIMO ZARIĆ · DRAGAN ZELENOVIĆ · ZORAN ŽIGIĆ

WANTED

WANTED

FATHER XMAS, FATHER XMAS, DON'T DEVIATE FROM YOUR PATH
Jasminko Arnautović and Juka Jaganjac
Tuzla, 1996

The title of this poster is drawn from a popular children's song. The signpost points to "Democracy, Multiculturalism, and Secularism."

In the winter of 1996, President Alija Izetbegović advised Muslims in Bosnia not to celebrate Christmas. Absurdly, several Bosnian men who dressed as Santa Claus were arrested. Most Muslims in Bosnia found this completely ludicrous. In the former Yugoslavia, and especially in Bosnia with its ethnically entwined population, celebrations for all the different faiths had been acknowledged by people of the other faiths. Bosnian Muslims almost unanimously ignored Izetbegović's appeal and it became much-lampooned. There was, however, a more serious side to Izetbegović's announcement: It indicated that the Bosnian leadership in Sarajevo tacitly recognized that Bosnia was now religiously and culturally divided.

OPPOSITE:
UNTITLED
Jasminko Arnautović and Juka Jaganjac
Tuzla, 1997

The poem by the distinguished Herzegovinian poet Mak Dizdar reads: "And the word for bread is bread / For wine is wine / For water is water."

Here Bosnia is being dismembered by three dragons that represent the forces of nationalism. The green Muslim dragon blindfolds the country while the other two kill it. The Croat dragon on the right stabs Bosnia in the back, and the Serb dragon cuts it up. Both posters on this spread were commissioned by the Tuzla Citizens' Forum.

Za riječ da hljeb je hljeb
Da vino je vino
A voda da je
Voda

CHOOSE THE BEST
TRIO
Sarajevo, 1996

This poster was commissioned by the OSCE (Organization
for Security and Cooperation in Europe), which is charged
with the organization and oversight of elections in Bosnia-
Herzegovina.

   The first postwar elections were held in September
1996. TRIO designed a series of posters of fruits and
vegetables with the same design format as this one. The
slogan asked voters across the country to ignore a
candidate's nationality and simply choose the best person
for the job.

   Although this campaign was widely ridiculed, it was
well intentioned. By eliminating all national symbols, the
OSCE wanted on the one hand to imply their own
impartiality, and on the other to encourage people to think
about the issue of nationalism.

OPPOSITE:
CHOOSE THE BEST
Samir Šestan
Lukavac, 1997

Polikita is a satirical magazine produced in Lukavac, near
Tuzla, parodying *Politika*, the main, state-controlled
newspaper in Serbia.

   Every issue of *Polikita* contains a free humorous poster.
At the time this one was designed there were still hundreds
of thousands of refugees abroad with no homes in Bosnia
to return to. Others, in Bosnia and elsewhere in the former
Yugoslavia, were desperate to leave the region.

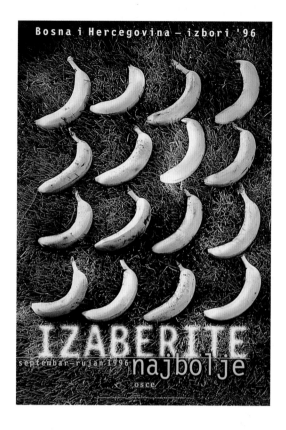

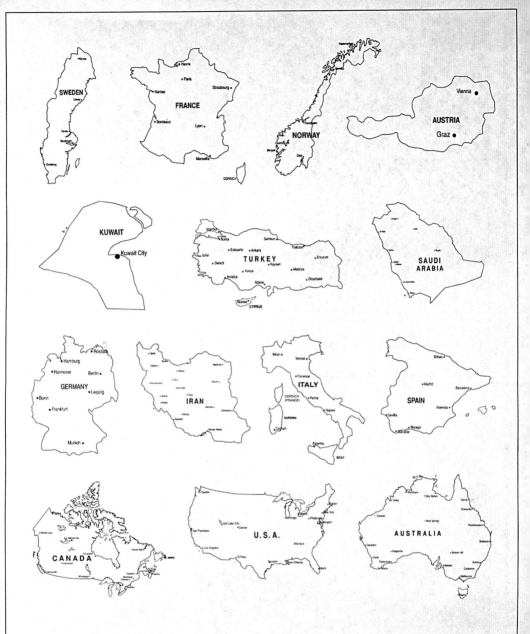

IZABERITE NAJBOLJE

SPONZOR PORUKE: OSCE

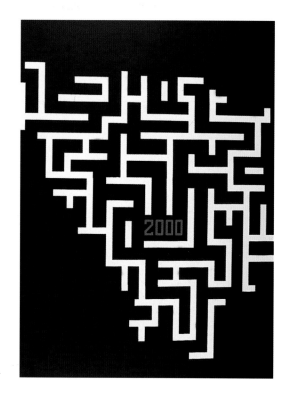

ABOVE LEFT:
UNTITLED
Šejla Kamerić
Sarajevo, 1996

ABOVE RIGHT:
UNTITLED
Dejan Vekić
Sarajevo, 1996

OPPOSITE:
UNTITLED
Samir Plasto
Sarajevo, 1996

The OHR (Office of the High Representative) is responsible for the civil administration of the Dayton agreement. In 1996 the OHR organized a poster competition, "Bosnia and Herzegovina 2000," asking for designs imagining the future of Bosnia. This poster, which was the winner, took car license plates as its theme. It deals with a serious problem that existed until 1998: Since each region of Bosnia issued its own license plates, the tags reflected the ethnicity of cars' drivers. Each of the three regions used a different national emblem, which seriously hindered freedom of movement in Bosnia.

Eventually the OHR introduced and enforced the use of a new, universal numbering system for cars.

MO 🏁 1996 HZ

BIH SA-1996 AA

CC 🦅 199-600

BIH ⁂ ? 2000

DESIGNPLASTOSAMIR96

POSTER COMPETITION OHR AND ALU
"BOSNIA & HERZEGOVINA 2000" July 1996.

OHR
Office of the
High Representative

BEWARE SNIPER (2000)
Alma Fazlić
Sarajevo, 1996

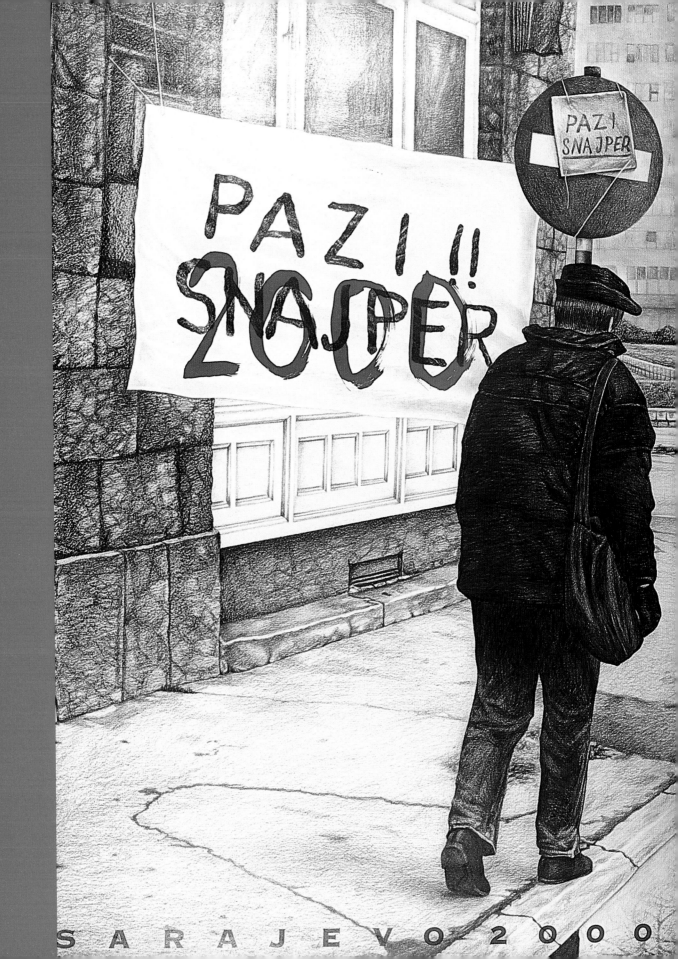

PAZI !! SNAJPER

SARAJEVO 2000

INDEX TO ARTISTS

DESIGN GROUPS, MAGAZINES, AND ORGANIZATIONS